AF807533

Learning From Precedent

Michael Bloch

BUILDING BLOCH BOOKS
NEW YORK CITY | 2012

A
BUILDING BLOCH BOOK
PAPERBACK

∞

Copyright © 2012 by Michael Bloch

All rights reserved. Except as permitted under the U.S. Copyright Act of 1976, no part of this publication may be reproduced, distributed, or transmitted in any form or by any means, or stored in a database or retrieval system, without the prior written permission of the publisher.

Building Bloch Books | New York, NY

For questions, comments, and requests, please email:
Books@BuildingBloch.Co

The Learning From Precedent name and art are trademarks of Building Bloch Books. The right of Michael Bloch to be identified as the author of this work has been asserted by him in accordance with the Copyright, Designs and Patents Act 1988.

ISBN 978-0-6156-3252-0

www.LearningFromPrecedent.com

For all students, regardless of whether law school is right for you

Table of Contents

Foreword by Sarah C. Zearfoss

Senior Assistant Dean for Admissions, Financial Aid, and Career Planning at the University of Michigan Law School

In the wake of the 2008 economic contraction, more attention than ever before is getting paid to the question of whether higher education is doing everything it ought for the people it aims to serve. And while it may be merely a question of myopia on my part, within that discussion, the focus on whether law school in particular is a sensible undertaking seems omnipresent.

Certainly, one ought to devote serious examination to whether any particular life course is worthy and appropriate before embarking on it. But what has been disconcerting to me in the current law school narrative is the dominant focus on whether law school is a value proposition, as judged solely from an economic point of view. Now, the capacity to earn a living wage from a given career—particularly when embarking on that career requires three years of post-graduate study and a substantial economic investment—is, as the philosophers would say, not unimportant. Yet, in thinking about the stories of my closest lawyer friends (and, to be perfectly honest, the vast majority of my closest friends are lawyers) and what led them to law school, money is never on the list of motivating factors. Usually, inspiration by lawyers from an earlier generation—Watergate, for example, occasioned many instances of both positive and negative inspiration—figures prominently. For my own part, I would say that 90% of what led me to law school was the example of my mother and her classmates, attending law school in the mid-1970s, many with the intention of changing of the world. (For my mother and the other women in her cohort, merely existing as lawyers at a time when only 3% of the bar were women itself changed the world, at least a little bit.)

The utility of focusing on considerations beyond income is doubtless why standard, and very valid, advice to anyone considering law school is: Talk to lawyers. Ask what they do, why they do it, whether they like it. After all, the role of income is relatively straightforward: you need to know what lawyers in particular fields earn, and compare it to what law school costs, and you can evaluate whether that's a satisfactory outcome for you. But as with a discussion of what led to law school in the first place, it is rare that I hear happy lawyers name their income on the short list of what makes them eager to get to work in the morning. Ability to make a difference, intellectual stimulation, variety of tasks—yes; monthly paycheck—no. Whatever they are, the items on those short lists are individual and particular, and thus a bit trickier to unearth.

Now, if you're already working in a legal environment, it's arguably easy enough to talk to a large number of lawyers about their career assessments and personal short lists, but you run a sampling error risk that talking only to people working for a single legal employer will lead to some invalid results. And if you're not already working with a critical mass of attorneys, chances are you're not going to be able to dig up more than one or two to talk to—a tiny dataset that statisticians would decry.

Enter Michael Bloch, solving these problems. After enterprisingly tackling the talking-to-lawyers project in the most thorough way I can imagine an individual doing, he's taken it upon himself to share the information with the world at large. How Mr. Bloch, as a junior at Berkeley, wrangled interviews with the president of the ACLU, the former governor of Michigan, the real-life Jerry Maguire, and the Judge Advocate General of the U.S. Navy, I cannot readily explain. I can only suppose that he is a master of the persuasive email. But there is no question that readers of the results will be exposed to both an incredibly wide range of post-law school careers and personality types.

Is it unreasonable to focus on the pinnacles of the profession in an effort to ascertain one's fit for what is likely to be a slightly more humdrum existence? Certainly, it's unrealistic to embark on law school if the only way you'll be satisfied with the results is by having one of the jobs described within this book. But while I hate the paean to ambition, "Shoot for the moon; even if you miss, you'll land among the stars" (because no, you won't; the stars are way, way, way farther away than the moon. Come on, people), there's a point there. Having a lofty goal as your polestar helps keep you on course for perhaps less lofty, but very laudable, attainments.

None of this is to counsel ignoring the negative. But there doesn't seem much danger of that, with a profusion of blogs and newspaper articles devoted to the cause. A short break from low-brow cynicism to indulge in a little high-toned inquiry isn't likely to annihilate your critical-thinking skills—and there's no doubt that because of Mr. Bloch, you'll gain exposure to lawyers that anyone, inside and outside of the profession, should find admirable.

Sarah Zearfoss
Ann Arbor, May 2012

Introduction

Are you trying to figure out what to do with your life after college? Are you considering law school? Are you wondering if law school is the best path to choose in achieving the goals you've set for yourself? I wrote *Learning From Precedent* with these questions in mind.

Since my freshman year in college, I have tried to determine whether law school is right for me. In the last few years, I joined various campus pre-law organizations, spent countless hours researching law schools online, and read numerous books and articles in an unfruitful attempt to reach a decision. Nothing seemed to help; though law school seemed like an appealing option, I couldn't be sure.

This year, I decided to ask for advice directly from the top law school graduates at my university. I hoped that hearing their frank thoughts on law school might allow me to unearth some new data points in my own decision-making. I took a chance on reaching out to a faculty member. She agreed to meet with me! And, in that meeting, I'd learned more about a future at law school than ever before. It struck me then that the best way to envision yourself on a path is to speak with those who have a head start. I figured I was not alone in weighing the decision of law school, and if speaking with others helped me, perhaps sharing these conversations with fellow students could better inform them about a future in which law school plays a part.

Each chapter in *Learning From Precedent* uncovers fascinating stories from some of America's most seasoned lawyers, and after hearing from their experiences, I hope you'll gain a better idea for your next steps. By identifying how they got to where they are, what they would do differently, and what advice they would give to students like you, *Learning From Precedent* is an exceptional resource to help you make your decision.

So, is law school right for *me*? With the help of these venerable professionals, I have made up my mind. (I'm holding my tongue until the Epilogue to share it with you). I hope you'll learn from the experts of *Learning From Precedent* as I did. Whether you want to be a politician, a titan of industry, a judge, or a screenwriter (or something else entirely!), *Learning From Precedent* will help you know if law school is for you.

With that, please enjoy *Learning From Precedent.*

Michael Bloch
Berkeley, June 2012

Interview I
THE SEC CHAIRMAN

David S. Ruder

David Ruder is a former Chairman of the Securities and Exchange Commission. He is a graduate of Williams College (1951) and received his Juris Doctor degree from the University of Wisconsin Law School (1957). He is Professor Emeritus and a former Dean at Northwestern University School of Law, founding chairman of the Securities and Exchange Historical Society, founding chairman of the Mutual Fund Directors Forum, and former partner and senior counsel at Baker & McKenzie.

Bloch: Where did you grow up?

Ruder: I grew up in a town called Wausau, Wisconsin. It was a small town of about 25,000 to 30,000 at that time. I went to Wausau High School, then to Williams College.

Bloch: What did you study at Williams?

Ruder: I was in the first Williams class that had a major in something called Political Economy. It was a combination major of Political Science and Economics. I actually started out as an Economics major, but I didn't have enough math background so I had to find something else. We had wonderful professors in the Political Science department, and wonderful professors in the Economics department, so I had very good training.

Bloch: Did you pick your major at Williams knowing that you wanted to go to law school?

Ruder: I wasn't set on becoming a lawyer when I went to Williams. I was taking whatever courses interested me. There was no thought of Economics or Political Science being something that would help me in law school. I just liked the subjects.

Bloch: So when did your interest in law first develop?

Ruder: My father was a lawyer in Wausau, so I always knew about law and decided to go into it after having served in the Korean War.

Bloch: And why corporate law?

Ruder: Specifically, my interest in corporate and securities law started when I went to practice law in Milwaukee after graduating from the University of Wisconsin Law School in '57. I was assigned a number of matters that spurred my interest, including one case that dealt with a rule of the Securities and Exchange Commission. When I went into law teaching, I continued my interest in corporate and securities matters.

Bloch: How would you summarize your experience in law school?

Ruder: I liked law school a lot, especially the experience of learning. I worked hard and was a very good student, and ended up graduating first in my law school class.

Law school was very good preparation for law practice. I took a wide variety of courses, in addition to six semesters of accounting while simultaneously attending law school. I accomplished that by going to summer school between my first and second years so I could pick up additional law school credits. I think the important part of going to law school, as well as college, is that you can get a broad background of courses that give you knowledge about life.

Bloch: Would you advise taking business law courses to anyone interested in corporate law?

Ruder: My main advice to a student who might become a corporate lawyer is to take a number of writing courses. Writing is key to the legal profession. In addition, I would advise taking courses in accounting, mathematics, and statistics. I did not come out of law school with a very strong mathematical background, but I would certainly suggest that someone thinking about a successful business career would be quite well off to have taken a fair dose of mathematics.

Bloch: What was the toughest part of your law school experience?

Ruder: Law school seemed natural to me. I think I had an advantage over my fellow students since I had spent three years in the service after graduating from Williams before entering law school.

I went through army basic training, and then through Officer Candidate School. It was in the army, particularly in basic training, that I learned there are lots of people in life who work with their hands, not their minds, and who don't understand the intellectual world. So I decided that when I got to law school, I was really going to work hard. I think that my attitude going into law school was a reflection of the maturity that came with having had three years away from undergraduate work before law school.

At Northwestern Law, where I'm currently Professor Emeritus, we have changed our admission requirements to reflect a preference for those who have had work experience. Today, over 90% of our students have had one or more years of work experience after college. Many students have had as many as three years of work experience. Most people are in a learning environment with no break from the time they start first grade until they finish college. They don't get an out-of-school experience to measure themselves by, which is invaluable.

I really think that I did well in law school because I was more emotionally mature and understanding of the need to work hard. I had the intellectual smarts to go with my work ethic, but I believe that my main success in life comes from being a hard worker, more so than being smart.

Bloch: In terms of your future career, what was the biggest value of going to law school?

Ruder: After practicing law, I came to Northwestern Law School as a professor, then dean. Eventually I became Chairman of the Securities and Exchange Commission. I would say that the biggest value of law school for all of those positions was the ability to see both sides of issues.

In law school you're taught that the law is not one-sided. The better lawyers not only understand the points on their side of the argument, but the points that the other side makes as well. Understanding opposing views allows you to be prepared to meet and rebut arguments.

I think that the ability to see both sides of a problem is also very beneficial to the businessperson. I've always thought that law is great training for business. If you can see both sides, you can anticipate problems that will arise when you follow your own inclinations.

That's not to say that there aren't downsides from training to be a lawyer. For example, some lawyers tend to become risk-averse because they see problems everywhere. To me, the ideal businessperson is someone who is willing to take risks, but can also recognize obstacles that are bound to arise.

Bloch: I've heard from many lawyers who say it's important to learn business, and from many businesspeople who say it's important to learn law. It seems as though the skill sets of the two professions are complementary.

Ruder: At a major law school like Northwestern, many of our graduates tend to go into the world of business, corporations, and commercial transactions. There are other areas of law such as estate planning, torts, criminal law, and property law that may not seem to involve business. I often find students who say, "I'm not interested in business law so I'm not taking any business courses." And I say to them, "Do you think your clients are never going to have any business interests? Shouldn't you be able to understand the business interests of that client? Shouldn't you be able to understand what obstacles those clients may have in becoming financially successful?" Sometimes I hear students say, "I don't want to be in business law. I want to go to trial." And I say, "What kind of cases will you be trying? Do you never plan on having a business case that you'll try?"

I think that avoiding business matters is wrong. The need to learn something about business is crucial for almost all types of law practice.

Bloch: Are there other sets of knowledge law school provides?

Ruder: I think that many people who have not gone to law school not only don't understand the nature of the legal process, but also don't know how historically the law became an alternative to war. In its simplest form, legal practice involves conflict resolution. In conflicts, each side has a different view. In the pre-law days, armies were sent out to decide conflicts. Eventually, lawyers became the combatants. In our legal system, the brightest legal minds, the best arguers, and the best thinkers come together to try to resolve conflicts.

Bloch: How did all of these understandings contribute to your career as a law school dean and as Chairman of the SEC?

Ruder: In some ways, I was fortunate to have been the dean of a law school before I became SEC Chairman. A dean has to deal with various constituencies—students, staff, professors, alumni, university administration, other departments, and other schools. I had a fair amount of experience dealing with these constituencies, and I was sensitive to the fact that each of them required attention.

As Chairman, similar responsibilities existed. I had to deal with investors, staff, other commissioners, Wall Street, Congress, the administration, and the press. In Washington, I quickly learned that no matter how much I thought I knew about something, I always had more to learn. I had some understanding of how Wall Street worked, but not a deep understanding of how individual large firms operated. I had a very steep learning curve, particularly when the stock market crashed only a few months after I arrived.

Bloch: Can you tell me about your time as Chairman? What motivated your move from academia?

Ruder: On the motivation side, as a professor I was interested in corporate and securities law. After 25 years or so as a law professor, I had become intensely involved in learning about securities regulation and securities markets. I had an abiding interest in the regulation of the purchase and sale of securities, in fraudulent conduct in the securities world, and in the operation of the securities markets. From my point of view—from a securities professor's point of view—when I was offered the opportunity to lead the organization I had been studying all my life, the answer was, "Yes!"

In terms of how I got there, the track was quite different than most people who become Chairman of the Securities and Exchange Commission. Most chairmen have some political connections and are active in a political party. I had no political background. I had begun by writing articles in the securities field. As a result of those articles, I was asked to speak. I spoke at a great number of securities meetings with lawyers. As a result of those speeches, I became active in the American Bar Association, and I served in its Business Law section. As a result of my various activities, I was asked to participate in a securities law project for the American Law Institute, the most learned of the legal organizations in the United States.

The then-Chairman of the SEC decided to retire after six years in the position. President Reagan looked for a suitable replacement from Wall Street and from regulators, but finally, decided to look at lawyers. Reagan's people began to ask around the White House, where many of the top people were lawyers. They asked for suggestions for Chairman of the SEC. It turned out that my name came up on almost all of the lists!

I think I was selected because of a combination of my reputation in the securities field from writing, speaking, and participating in activities of the American Bar Association, and my work in the academic world as a dean. I don't advertise this, but I knew that I wasn't a political candidate, so I called myself the "competency candidate" instead!

Bloch: What was it like being the Chairman?

Ruder: Being Chairman of the SEC was, to use modern vernacular, a 24/7 job. I remember when I went into the office for the first time, I asked, "How much vacation do I get?" My staff looked at me and said, "Mr. Chairman"—that name gets to be very exciting—"Mr. Chairman, you work all the time! You can take all the vacation you want, but you'll always be working!" Indeed, in my time as a lawyer, professor, dean, and Chairman, I have tended to work very hard.

My work at the SEC was extremely exciting, but one thing that I was not well prepared for was dealing with the press. The newspapers were the main mode of communication back in the '80s. I found that the press was not very friendly. Members of the press always wanted to know more, regardless of what you wanted to tell them, and they were always looking for things that were wrong.

As far as the press is concerned, that part of the job hasn't changed. The press doesn't always report accurately on what happens, and sometimes you even think that there is bias in the reporting. I had to learn to be very, very careful with the press and not say the wrong thing, or say too much, so I would not be misreported. It was a great wake-up call for me.

Bloch: Having been in academia, the public sector, and the private sector, which do you enjoy the most?

Ruder: Enjoy is a particularly interesting word. The most exciting, all-encompassing position I've ever had was Chairman of the SEC. You are totally immersed intellectually. You're working with a group of dedicated people toward a common objective: the public good, protecting the markets and investors.

You have a chance to affect outcomes. The SEC is an independent regulatory agency. All of the commissioners are nominated by the President and confirmed by the Senate. They cannot be easily removed by the President, so essentially they are independent of the White House. The President doesn't call the SEC Chairman to tell the SEC what to do. On the other hand, the SEC must persuade both the President and Congress to provide an adequate budget, so it's not entirely independent. Nevertheless, the SEC has great autonomy in getting things done.

It's quite different than academia. As a professor, it's a thrill to teach students and to be appreciated by them. You're excited about the law and write scholarly articles, but you don't have an immediate effect on events. In my time at the SEC, we had to deal with the stock market crash and enforcement cases, including insider trading and financial fraud. We had to interact with the international world and we had to ensure that corporations were providing information to the public. It was a heady time in terms of the ability to accomplish things. It was really the best time in my life.

The SEC was a very, very hard job. I was exhausted when I came out. I was happy enough to leave, although my time had been wonderful. Because I was Chairman of the SEC, I have had a number of fascinating *pro bono* public interest assignments. I was a member of the Board of Governors of the National Association of Securities Dealers—now called FINRA—one of the self-regulators of the securities markets. I became a member of the Financial Accounting Foundation which oversees promulgation of Generally Acceptable Accounting Principles [GAAP] in the United States. I became a member of a similar foundation in London, where we oversaw the creation of international accounting standards. Then I became founding chairman of the Securities and Exchange Commission Historical Society, which chronicles the history of the SEC. Most recently I've been the founding chairman of the Mutual Fund Directors Forum, which provides education to independent directors of mutual funds.

My SEC experience led to a lot of other work and to a very interesting post-SEC life. I've been lucky to continue to be very active intellectually.

Bloch: Do you have any additional advice for students hoping to become the future Chairman of the SEC?

Ruder: You can aspire to be the SEC chairman, but life doesn't work in a straight line. My advice for a student is to work hard. Do as many intellectual things as you like to do and as well as you can. Put one foot in front of the other and see where life leads you.

At the same time, I think it's important that one learns how to have regard for other people. You need to understand that every person in life is important. You have to respect others' values. I think getting along in business or government requires that understanding. Most important, as I tell my children, I believe the number one path to happiness and success is honesty and integrity. If you are honest and tell the truth, people will respect you and they will trust you. Believe me, trust is extremely important in life.

So, my advice for students is to work hard, do what you're interested in, be honest, and follow what life gives you. There will be opportunities that come. I rarely turned down an offer to participate in a meeting or give a speech. That led to being invited to do other things, including being invited to be Chairman of the SEC. Success in one space gives you momentum toward something else. Reputational progress that you gain by being honest, working hard, and doing a good job will follow you everywhere.

Interview II
THE ACTIVIST

Susan N. Herman

Susan Herman was elected the President of the American Civil Liberties Union in 2008 and has been a Centennial Professor of Law at Brooklyn Law School since 1980. She is a graduate of Barnard College (1968), and received her Juris Doctor degree from New York University School of Law (1974) where she was a Note and Comment Editor on the Law Review. She is the author of "The Right to a Speedy and Public Trial" (2006), the co-author of "Terrorism, Government, and Law: National Authority and Local Autonomy in the War on Terror" (2008), and most recently, "Taking Liberties: The War on Terror and the Erosion of American Democracy" (2011).

Bloch: Where are you from?

Herman: I grew up on Long Island in New York. My father was a lawyer and my mother was a legal secretary at his office, which is how they met.

Bloch: Did your parents encourage your interest in law?

Herman: It's hard to say. I never thought I would go to law school after college because I wanted to go into theater. After I finished my undergrad studying philosophy at Barnard, I tried to find a way into the theater world. That didn't work out as quickly as I expected, so I ended up taking a job in publishing. I worked at an arts-related magazine as an editorial assistant and quickly worked my way up to be the Editor-in-Chief. It was a lot of fun, but I had an "attack of relevance" of sorts and felt that law school was where I needed to be.

Bloch: Was that easier or harder than the path most law school students take?

Herman: I think that having a few years off before law school was a pretty helpful thing for me. Having done something else between college and law school gave me a clearer idea of what I wanted out of the experience.

Back when I went to law school, the admissions director once said, "Some of you are in law school because you couldn't handle medical school. Some of you are here because you're on a big academic choo-choo train and you didn't know where to get off." The idea was that when you see yourself as just a student and wait for the people in the front of the room to tell you what to do, it's not the best way to approach law school. I think it's much better if you have a sense of what you want to do in the law, and why you're interested in it. If you do that, you can make the most of the opportunities that become available to you.

Bloch: Are there any examples of opportunities that came to you because you didn't go straight into law school after college?

Herman: One of the things that happened while I was in law school was that I got to spend a lot of time working with one of my professors who was involved with the ACLU. I had signed up to be a research assistant, and ended up assisting on a big case he was working on that ended up going all the way to the Supreme Court.

There were six graduate students at Stony Brook University who shared a house in a little village on Long Island named Belle Terre. The village had this little beach, so when summer came along, the students went to get their beach permit from the village. They were told that they couldn't get one because they were illegal residents! What they hadn't known was that the village had a zoning ordinance that said the whole village was zoned only for single-family houses, and a family was defined as "no more than two persons unrelated by blood, marriage, or adoption." So pretty surprising.

The students came to see my professor, Lawrence Sager, who at the time was working with the New York Civil Liberties Union. We ended up filing a federal court complaint on their behalf, and we asked the judge to order that they couldn't be evicted or prosecuted for violation of the ordinance while the court was considering whether or not this law was constitutional. The judge signed the order and wrote in by hand that the students should be allowed to go to the beach.

I went out to Belle Terre to talk to the students and update them about the case. When they were showing me around the vicinity, we went to see the beach, and the moment our tires hit the parking lot, this big man comes striding across the lot, comes up to us, and says, "What are you doing here? You're not allowed here!" So the students look at me like I'm in charge, and I take out the federal court order and show it to him. He looked at it, looked at me, and melted. And I thought, "This is cool! I want to do this."

Bloch: It seems like you never really left the ACLU afterwards.

Herman: I always felt connected in a way. After law school, I took a Pro Se clerkship. Most law clerks are called "elbow clerks"—you literally sit next to a judge's elbow—but in a Pro Se clerkship, you take care of petitions and motions from all the people who are litigating without lawyers. ["Pro se" means by or for oneself]. So I didn't work for a particular judge, but I worked on Pro Se petitions.

Whenever we had memos finished, we would present them to whatever judges were on duty for the week. Our portfolio was very interesting to me because people without lawyers tend to be civil rights plaintiffs—the prisoners, the *habeas corpus* cases, the kinds of people whose stories I found compelling. My job was to be somewhat sympathetic to them. They weren't lawyers, they weren't professionals, so what we looked to see was if they really had a legal claim. I liked that job because it wasn't just being an objective court, it was a little bit of being an advocate for those people as well.

Bloch: Is that what got you interested in this type of law?

Herman: I think what forms our values and predilections often goes way back. Here's the story that I tell when people ask where my civil liberties values come from. You asked me earlier if I was interested in law because my father was a lawyer. The earliest memory that I have of a particular incident that helped to shape my attitudes involves not my father but my non-lawyer mother.

When I was in third grade at Long Beach Elementary School, in Long Beach, New York, our class play was *Johnny Tremain,* which is about a boy in the American Revolutionary War. We were doing this play, and since plays don't have as many words as books, I thought it would be interesting to take the novel out of the school library. I go to the library to check out the book, and the librarian tells me that I'm not allowed to because the book is in the boy's section.

I knew that there was a girl's section and a boy's section because I had read just about all the things in the girl's section, which had a very limited repertoire—mostly fairy tales or biographies of presidents' wives. So I accepted this rebuff and went home and told my mom about it. She was furious. She called somebody at the school and told them that they should let me take out that book, and any other book I wanted.

It was my first civil liberties eye-opener—to see that someone in authority might actually be doing something wrong by telling me what I was supposed to read. And seeing my mother standing up to that made a great impression.

I think an early experience of seeing the world in a certain way—promoting self-reliance, instead of "the authority is always right," for example—can really influence one's world view. It wasn't just that one experience for me. I think it was my mother's point of view in general. She showed me that there was a possibility you could say to the school library, "You're wrong. I should be able to make my own decisions about what to read."

Bloch: Is that why you chose the ACLU over another organization that does a similar thing?

Herman: That's a question I love. What I treasure about the ACLU is that we connect the dots. What the ACLU is all about is that a denial of equality to one person or one group is offensive to everybody.

Just today actually I was talking at a United Sikhs Conference. They love the ACLU because we defend their rights when they have problems, but I think they also appreciate the fact that we also represent Muslims, Christians, Jews, and Rastafarians. Because it's all the same thing. It's all about the golden rule. The basic concept is not, "I should have rights because I'm me and I want what's good for me," but rather, "I should respect someone else's rights because I want them to respect mine."

That's what I love about being affiliated with a multi-issue organization. We have all these very different people involved, who represent groups of people who have very distinct concerns: not just freedom of speech and religion but reproductive freedom, voting rights, immigrants' rights, the fairness of the criminal justice system, and so on. Just this weekend I chaired an ACLU Board meeting. We have 82 people on the Board, and you wouldn't believe how diverse this group is. There are people who were in the civil rights movement who now focus on LGBT rights, because they recognize that it's all part of the same battle against intolerance. There are people who passionately oppose the death penalty who also get that it's just a variation of unfairness when people with disabilities suffer discrimination. Everyone's various issues about discrimination or injustice are at bottom the same issues.

Bloch: Where does that philosophy stem from?

Herman: I think that philosophy is really grounded in the Constitution. The foundational principles of our nation are truly great principles. If you look at the Bill of Rights, you read that you have freedom of speech and freedom of religion. Those provisions promise us that the government can't tell us what to think or what to be, and that each of us has the opportunity and the responsibility to make those decisions for ourselves.

A number of provisions in the Constitution make important statements about the relationship between the government and an individual. These are our nation's fundamental principles. And implementing those principles is what we're here to do. The ACLU's slogan is "Because freedom can't defend itself."

Bloch: Looking at where you are now, as President of the ACLU, do you still feel like you get to take a hands-on role in this mission? Or is it more of a management position?

Herman: That's a very preceptive question. For years before becoming President I was General Counsel to the ACLU. There I definitely used my specific legal training—I worked on briefs and actual cases. I don't do as much law anymore. What I'm doing instead is various management roles: I run Board meetings, I make sure the budget is in order, and I ensure the Board is functioning.

Another thing I do is communications, speaking on behalf of the organization. I meet with people who are supporters, people who disagree with us—all different kinds of groups. As I mentioned, earlier today I spoke with a group of Sikhs. Next week I'm speaking to the Connecticut Library Association. I've spoken at the U.S. Army War College. I speak at many different places so that I can talk to people about current threats to our civil liberties and help them understand what the ACLU actually does. I wrote a book explaining the impact of our domestic anti-terrorism policies on ordinary Americans [*Taking Liberties*]. So you're right that it's a different role, but I don't feel like I'm no longer on the front lines. It's just a different front line.

Bloch: Would you say that the skills and experiences you have from law school really help you in your current position, or were they more applicable while serving as General Counsel?

Herman: I'd say both. I have friends from law school who ended up not really practicing law. But they'll still tell you that they use their legal training all the time. It's a very disciplined way of approaching problems.

There is a connection to my philosophy undergraduate major too; I think a lot of the law is very much related to syllogistic logic, or the ability to follow structures of arguments. I think my philosophy training was very important to my ability to analyze arguments, but I think my legal training was as well.

Since the ACLU is involved in so many distinct civil liberties and civil rights issues, we have to consider and develop policies in many different areas. I always empathize with people who are not lawyers because it can be very hard to follow what you want your position to be when First Amendment or search and seizure questions, for example, can require mastering very complex legal interpretations of the Constitution. So yes, I use my legal training in approaching any question. It's part of who I am.

Bloch: Does that alienate you from the rest of the population?

Herman: I think there are two different planes of what you might call alienation. One is that lawyers are trained to develop a mindset that other people don't always get.

For example, I live in a co-op, which is when a number of neighbors co-own a building. The co-op board has to approve every new tenant who comes in. One of my neighbors was about to move and planned on selling his unit to somebody else. He called us up to let us know that he had found a great person to buy the apartment. My husband and I said,

"Well, that's nice, but we'll still have to have a meeting of the co-op board to approve the buyer." And this guy was really offended. He said, "Well, why do you think I'd sell the apartment to someone who wouldn't be a good neighbor? I paid attention to that. Why is it necessary to have a hearing? Why don't you trust me?"

I get that he didn't understand the importance of the approval process, but to me it's so clear. That's the nature of procedure—it's not personal, but a structure that can help decide questions in a way that is fair rather than personal. That's why we have criminal trials even when the people involved are absolutely sure they know who did it. Due process is important. As a lawyer I really believe in process, and at times, I do think that can be an alienating point of view, even though I think it's the correct one.

A lot of people say, for instance, "who cares if we're sending a targeted drone to kill an American when we know he's a terrorist." And I stop and say, "Wait, he may be a very bad person, but you need a process because one day there will be a situation where you think you know a target's guilty, but you're wrong." And that's what fair process is all about. One could call this insistence on taking proper steps instead of rushing to judgment alienating because not everyone gets it, but I think it's just an essential way of being careful.

Bloch: And the second plane of alienation?

Herman: People often ask me why the ACLU is so unpopular in some circles, and I think it's built into the territory. The way the Constitution works, it gives us all these rights despite what a majority of people think. The idea is that because you have a constitutional right, if that right is limited by a law or action that's supported by a majority, you can come to the courts, invoke the Consitution, and hope to be vindicated.

For example, Sikhs, the group I spoke to today, have problems all over the country because people want them to take off their turbans. Not everyone understands that this is a religious obligation. So the Sikhs come to ACLU offices around the country and say, "Our neighbors don't understand. The police want us to take off our turbans. They made me leave the courtroom because I wouldn't take it off. They wouldn't hire me for a job because I wear a turban." You see all sorts of discrimination because people are not accustomed to accommodating this unfamiliar religion.

Because everyone should have equal rights to exercise their religion, it is our job to defend the people who have unfamiliar religions and who therefore encounter problems, like the Sikhs. We don't have occasion to represent Christians or Jews or other mainstream religions on free exercise claims quite as often, because it doesn't often happen that laws or government officials make it difficult for a Catholic to use rosary beads, for example, or force people to work on Christmas. So what happens is that we find often ourselves representing religions that are less understood—and, by the same token, speech that is unpopular.

Bloch: What type of speech?

Herman: If you stand on a street corner and say, "America is the greatest place ever and I love apple pie," no one is going to try to stop you. You're only going to have a problem when you're saying something that a lot of people don't want to hear. We ended up representing groups like the Nazi party, for example, because when they want to have their parades, people say, "No, they can't say those ugly things because people will get upset." It's the unpopular speech that we find ourselves having to go to bat for, and not everybody understands why that's right and necessary.

To me, it's right there in the Constitution. The government can't tell you what to say. They can't tell you what religion to have. You get to choose. Your neighbors can't make you say what they think or follow their religion. No one can judge your choice and say, "It's the wrong religion," or "I think that's a stupid thing to say, so you can't say it" or "You can't have a parade to express that point of view." And therefore, our work is very often on behalf of minorities and underdogs—racial minorities, viewpoint minorities, and religious minorities. We try our best to be viewpoint neutral.

So as to the word "alienating," a lot of people just really don't understand that the ACLU is standing up for fundamental American values. I get hate mail. I get it from Christians who say, "Why is the ACLU anti-Christian?" which of course we're not. We've had many cases where we represent Christians, like the high school valedictorian whose school told her she couldn't speak in her address about the centrality of her faith in her life. People see us defending individuals or groups that are different or unpopular, which to some seems un-American. There are people who think it's better to have a community where everyone has the same religion, says the same things, and lives in a family with mom and dad and the kids. But I don't think that's the vision of the Constitution.

I think the ACLU is here to defend the multicultural, individualistic aspect of what it means to be an American. We all have the right to make our own choices. If people feel threatened by the choices of others, this level of tolerance may seem alienating, but I think it's also what the Constitution and our mission are all about.

Bloch: How does it feel representing people with whom you may disagree?

Herman: It's kind of a lawyerly distinction that not everybody finds easy. You're supporting somebody's right to speak even if you don't agree with them. Sometimes we're in a position where I feel like I have to hold my nose to defend someone's right to say something I think is disgusting.

I'll give you the most recent example. The Supreme Court recently made a decision in a case involving the Westboro Baptist Church. What a horrible thing to do—to go to funerals of fallen soldiers and blame their deaths on the United States not being homophobic enough. It's disgraceful on every level. They may be doing it just to get publicity, but they are upsetting bereaved families and promoting hate. But when a governmental entity says to them, "You can't say that," we have to take the position that the government can't just repress free speech because we don't like its content. The ACLU said the same thing about war protesters in World War I, and we say the same thing about abortion clinic demonstrations. Even if we don't agree with them, people who want to protest and say that abortion is murder have the right to do that.

In either case, the First Amendment does allow reasonable "time, place, and manner" restrictions to make sure that protestors are not right in the face of families at a funeral or a woman who wants to have an abortion. But you can't say, "That's a disgusting message so you can only say that two miles away." That's not right. If the First Amendment means anything, it means people can say things that are upsetting. And there again, there are people who have a hard time accepting that.

People will say, "I understand the First Amendment, but we should be able to make an exception for just this one thing, because it's too disgusting and will really make some people feel bad." But then someone will want an exception for hate speech. Someone else will want it for Holocaust denial. And adding up all those exceptions would swallow the First Amendment. So you can't go down the road of making just a few exceptions, because it's a really slippery slope. The rule has to be that the government can't censor speech on the basis of its content.

Is it always easy to take this principled position? No. I was actually at the Supreme Court for another argument when the Court announced its ruling in the Westboro case. There were a number of people from the ACLU there. We all looked at each other, and no one was celebrating. Our emotions were mixed, but we all rationally thought, "Well, they were right to say that." And I think it's important in the long run to encourage free speech.

Oliver Wendell Holmes used to say that speech is a marketplace of ideas. Ultimately, we hope that good speech will drive out the bad speech. If you let the bad speech come to light, other people can draw attention to what's wrong with it. And people will begin to understand that. If you try to suppress the speech, it can fester.

Bloch: I must say I don't think I ever fully appreciated the position that you're in, or the range of difficulties and challenges that you face.

Herman: Sometimes there's a case that an individual lawyer will just have a problem with. Sometimes it's just really hard to follow principle over emotion. I think we all really believe in one of the essential principles of the Anglo-American criminal justice system, for example—that you should be willing to let ten guilty people go free to avoid convicting one innocent person. Sometimes it's hard and you don't want to do it, but you have to do it consistently for the integrity of the system.

Bloch: So given all of this, what's a piece of advice you'd give to an undergrad who's thinking about working for the ACLU or another activist organization?

Herman: Many people in my generation grew up with a very strong sense that we didn't want to work just for money but for results we cared about—like promoting civil rights. As I told you, I had a very nice career in publishing and it was fun, but I didn't feel that I was contributing to social justice and so I just didn't feel that I was really doing something that mattered. To me, the idea that I get up every morning and truly believe I'm working for justice, that I'm doing something that matters, makes a tremendous difference.

There's a Bob Dylan song that says, "Everybody's got to serve somebody." There are a lot of people I know who really love their work because they're serving somebody or something they believe in. I don't think that everybody will find their motivation in the quest for social justice, or that everybody needs to. Take artists who love the process of making their art. They may not be serving some grander social ideal and there's nothing wrong with that. There are lawyers who just love the intricacies of the tax code. But I think everybody deserves to think that what they are doing matters, whether they love the process or the potential results.

Find something you're passionate about. Find whatever it is that will motivate you and make you want to get up in the morning and make you feel you're really making a difference. It might be law, it might be something else, but I think everybody has the right to feel good about what they're doing in life. The concept of life, liberty, and the pursuit of happiness can apply to careers too.

Interview III
THE PATENT PROSECUTOR

Sean M. Dean

Sean Dean is a Principal in the Boston office of Fish & Richardson. Dr. Dean studied mathematics at Duke University (1987) and received his MSE, Ph.D., and Juris Doctor degrees from the University of Michigan in 1993, 1998, and 2004, respectively. Dr. Dean's practice emphasizes patent prosecution and counseling, opinion work, due diligence studies, and development and management of patent portfolios. Dr. Dean served as an officer in the U.S. Navy since 1987 before retiring from the U.S. Navy Reserves as a Commander in 2008.

Bloch: Tell me about yourself.

Dean: I'm from West Virginia. For college, I attended Duke, majoring in mathematics on a Navy ROTC scholarship.

Bloch: Why did you decide to join the Navy?

Dean: My high school counselor told me that I needed to apply for a Navy scholarship. Although at first not interested, after seeing what the Navy had to offer, I realized it was a great program and something I was interested in experiencing.

In Navy ROTC, I spent one month each summer doing something in the actual service. My first summer I flew over to Germany, got on a ship, and spent a week out in the North Sea, a week in Denmark, and ten days coming back to Boston. I loved being at sea and thought the experience was great. I ended up going through with it and became a Surface Warfare Officer, which essentially means I was a ship-driver.

Bloch: What made you interested in getting a law degree?

Dean: It was a long route for me. I studied mathematics as an undergraduate, and after going through my post-Navy options, settled on engineering. I really liked the subject and thought it was a great way to leverage math with interesting work that has the potential to make the world a better place. I ended up in the doctoral program in Environmental Engineering at Michigan, where I did work on water resources and site remediation.

The first time I thought about law was during graduate school. During my first summer, I worked in a large company's environmental quality office. While there, I got to work closely with environmental lawyers. Previously, it was my perception that lawyers caused problems, not solved them. I thought they would look for loopholes so that companies didn't have to spend as much money or energy trying to clean things up.

In actuality, it was the reverse. The engineers were looking at regulations and seeing the most efficient ways to meet them—if it's good enough to meet the requirements, it's a good solution. Rather than looking for loopholes, the lawyers were focused on getting things really cleaned up even if it cost more time, money, and energy because they felt that anything left in the ground was a future potential liability.

It was an interesting switch in my perception. As a result, I considered switching from engineering to law. But I had my fellowship and liked what I was doing, so I decided to stay and get my doctorate.

Bloch: What about after the doctorate?

Dean: After I got my doctorate, I headed down to Florida to work on site remediation. I liked my job and the people I was working with, but what I liked best was working with other stakeholders and looking at regulations and how they applied on-site. Negotiating with stakeholders to bring parties with different interests together to a common technical solution was my favorite part of the job. I worked alongside environmental lawyers, and their jobs focused on the parts of my job that I enjoyed the most.

At the time, I was planning on teaching [standardized testing] review classes to help pay for my student loans. Having a family on an engineer's salary was tough. I assumed I would teach GRE courses, but when I applied for the job, the staff told me, "We already have a lot of GRE teachers, but you did really well on the verbal and logic portions, why not teach the LSAT?" So all of a sudden I started thinking about what an environmental lawyer really does and I remember thinking to myself, "Hey, this is pretty cool." I ended up taking the LSAT, did well, and started considering going back to school.

At that point of my career, my wife and I already had four kids. We knew law school was going to be very disruptive so I spoke to everyone I knew who had become lawyers to find out what their jobs were like. Did they like it? What did they do? Would they do it again, if they could? Kind of like the process you're doing—but at 35-years-old.

I found that a lot of lawyers didn't like their jobs. A lot of them were incredibly unhappy and thought law school was especially tough. However, it seemed like people with technical backgrounds had somewhat of an easier time. Same thing for people with military backgrounds. Whether it's just time management or a different way of thinking that is learned from previous endeavors, they had an easier time of it.

Bloch: Was it like that for you?

Dean: Yes, it was. If you end up going to law school, it's all about time management. For me, law school was like a job. I went in at 8 a.m., I went home at 6 p.m. Sometimes, I worked after the kids were in bed. Because I did that from the start, it was never a big deal, but others would say, "Nothing is due now, so I'll go out late and sleep in." Trying to backload work is not successful. If you work at it from the start, it's much more manageable.

I did enjoy law school though. It's definitely longer than what it needs to be for lawyers to go out and practice. A lot of law schools, especially the academically focused programs like Michigan, do a great job of preparing people to be academics and clerks for judges. However, the practice of law is not the focus for most classes.

Bloch: Once you were at law school, what was the toughest part of being there?

Dean: There wasn't one toughest part. It's all hard work. There's never a moment when you say, "I'm sure I can do this." Structurally, it's different. It's hard to adjust to the fact that most classes are based on just one data point: how well you do on the final exam. You're not getting feedback along the way. The first semester you may feel like you get what you're doing, that you have the hang of it, but there's no way to get concrete feedback.

Bloch: How did you end up in patent rather than environmental law?

Dean: One of the people I spoke to when considering switching to law was a friend from high school who told me he loved being a lawyer. I asked him what he did that was different than all the other lawyers who seemed to dislike their jobs. It turns out, he was a patent lawyer.

Patent law builds on my experiences. I'm not a patent litigator—litigators are out suing people about patents—I'm a patent prosecutor and counselor. I help people get patents and help them decide what they should spend their time, energy, and money on protecting.

Eight years in, I completely agree with him. I'm always learning new things. I work with creative people who are at the top of their fields. It's a diversity of practice that helps keep it fresh.

Bloch: What was the biggest value of getting your law degree?

Dean: For me, the most important thing was the credentials that I got with the piece of paper. You also learn how to learn. You may have gotten that from earlier experiences, but in law school you get a broad grounding in your first year so that you can go over material quickly and identify the issues that need to be considered.

Bloch: Would you say that skill is the most helpful thing to your career at Fish & Richardson?

Dean: No, I think having a solid foundation of legal skills as a baseline is important but everyone who practices law has a foundation of legal skills. The most important things are your depth of analysis, your ability to manage your time, and your ability to communicate with colleagues and clients.

Lawyers have the skill set and knowledge to understand consequences and what laws and regulations mean, but more than that, we serve as translators and advocates. We have more to do than we have time to do. Being able to prioritize projects and manage time is extremely important to survival and success in any law practice.

Bloch: What is one piece of advice you would give to an undergraduate who is thinking of becoming a patent prosecutor?

Dean: You've got to have a technical background. If you're thinking about becoming a patent prosecutor, try it out first. Firms often hire people to work as clerks, so if you're thinking about taking the patent bar, first get some practical experience at a patent firm. It's important to make sure you understand what you're getting yourself into and to make sure you like it.

That circles back to what you're doing and what I did. Make sure you understand the choices that you make before you invest time, energy, and money into three years of law school. You don't yet know what you're going to do as a lawyer. I ended up doing something very different than what I initially thought I would do. It's hard and expensive, and people need to be realistic about what their opportunities are on the backside, and whether those opportunities are work the investment and will lead to something they want to spend their lives doing.

Bloch: Would you change anything about the path you took or the timeline you did it in?

Dean: I love where I'm at now, so I would be hesitant to change anything. But if I could change one thing, I would have gone to law school right after my master's degree. If I had done that, I would be eight to ten years further along in my career. I'm glad I did what I did and I had fun along the way, but it would be nice to be further along.

Bloch: So the Ph.D. isn't necessary for going into this practice?

Dean: It depends what technical field you're in. The people in life sciences who do genetics or high-level biology, they—at least at FR [Fish & Richardson]—need at least a master's degree and four to five years of industry experience, or a doctorate. For the mechanical side—I'm an environmental engineer, but I mostly do mechanical patent work—there are advantages to a Ph.D., but it's not a necessity. We have people here with just a Bachelor or Master in Mechanical Engineering.

Bloch: Any final advice in terms of deciding whether or not law school is right for you?

Dean: I want to reiterate that people who are considering going to law school should talk to lawyers in fields that they're likely to work in. There is a tendency for people to think that practicing law is like what's on TV or what they read in papers about lawyers at big firms. But that's not reflective of what most lawyers do.

Once you take the LSAT and figure out where you're going for law school, talk to people who have graduated from that school and ask them about what they're doing. Do they like it? Would they rather be doing something else? Remember that there are a lot of opportunities out there and a lot of open doors.

Interview IV
THE JUDGE

Jeremy D. Fogel

Jeremy Fogel is the 10th Director of the Federal Judicial Center in Washington D.C. He graduated from Stanford University (1971) and received his Juris Doctor degree from Harvard Law School (1974). Fogel was nominated by President William J. Clinton to a seat on the United States District Court for the Northern District of California in 1997, and was confirmed by the United States Senate in 1998. His most prominent case involved challenges to California's procedures for lethal injection, a practice that he halted in 2006 after finding flaws in the state's execution process. In October 2011, Chief Justice John G. Roberts, Jr., who chairs the Board of the Federal Judicial Center, announced Judge Fogel's selection.

Bloch: Can you tell me about your childhood?

Fogel: I was born in San Francisco, but my family moved to Southern California when I was five. My dad was a trial lawyer, and my mom, who had a business degree, worked in different management capacities. When my brother and I were growing up though, she stayed at home.

Bloch: Where did you go for college?

Fogel: I went to Stanford for undergrad, where I majored in religious studies. The subject really appealed to me. As a freshman, I had taken a couple types of classes—just shopping around—but I found the whole topic of religious studies very interesting. Learning about what people ultimately care about and how they find meaning in their lives I found enormously exciting.

Since it was a very small program—there were only about 25 people in it—I had a lot of chances to work up close with wonderful professors and study the things I really cared about.

Bloch: That doesn't seem like a typical route to law school.

Fogel: It was not that typical. I didn't meet many other people of that background when I got to law school.

Bloch: How then did you first become interested in law?

Fogel: My dad was a lawyer, so I was certainly aware of what the legal profession was like for him. Then, what I found in college was that even though I was interested in broader philosophical questions that you don't normally run into in the law, it seemed to me that the way people actually find meaning in the world is through human relations. Law was a way to do something helpful, to do public service. Law seemed to me to be a service profession; one where I could express myself and could meet my need to help others.

Bloch: Is that why you wanted to be a judge?

Fogel: When I was in college, and even when I was in law school, I never thought of becoming a judge. It's definitely not a career that I aspired to. What happened was that after I finished law school at Harvard, I saw how pretentious and adversarial the legal system could be. I recognized that where my talent and my interests lie was in working through problems, getting people to communicate better with each other, and helping them better understand the other's side.

The role of an advocate, where I had to demonize my opponent or build up my side to be better than it was, is one that I was uncomfortable with. The role of being someone who could bring people together to try and find where reason lies, to try and find a way to reconcile people's interests, that was something I realized is more suited for a judge.

Another thing that influenced it was my experience working as a mental health advocate. Most of my clients were extremely vulnerable people. I found that some judges—certainly not all, there were some very fine judges that I appeared before—were disrespectful of my clients and seemed to not have the patience or understanding to see how important their role was. It was this type of negative inspiration, seeing some bad examples, that made me say, "You know, this is something where I can really see myself making a difference."

I did see good examples, some great judges who always treated people respectfully and maintained the dignity of the court. I was inspired by that. Somewhere along the process of being a lawyer I just realized it's something I wanted to do. But I was well into my law career before I came to that realization.

Bloch: What was your experience in law school actually like?

Fogel: It was difficult. Law school was very challenging. I feel like a lot of what goes on is a socialization process. The school quite intentionally tried to get us to think in a particular way. Not to have us get to a certain political philosophy or anything like that, but just to think the way lawyers think and learn the way lawyers learn.

That's not a bad thing. If you're going to be a lawyer it's good to know how lawyers think, but I felt that it narrowed our perspectives too much. It caused us to focus on certain kinds of things to the exclusion of others, like the experience of clients, people who are actually represented by lawyers and appear in court. The training is such that we as lawyers could analyze issues and present good arguments and write good briefs, but we didn't learn how to listen to people and understand what was motivating our clients so that we could be helpful to them in the fullest possible way. We learned how to be helpful to them in a particular system with a particular set of assumptions. I found that to be frustrating. I felt that then and I feel that now. It's narrower than how things actually are.

Bloch: Would you say that was the toughest part of your law school career?

Fogel: I think so. Just dealing with that mindset. I did find ways to compensate for it. I worked part-time at a mental health unit and a crisis intervention center. That's how I got into the mental health field. I worked with people who could care less about the law; they just needed somebody to help them through a crisis or listen to what they had to say. I think that with that additional perspective, and some good friends, it was fine.

When I look back on it, I think I really got a great legal education. I believe I was trained very well, even though the process of going through it, as I said before, is a narrowing experience. Consciously so.

Bloch: Do you think that is starting to change in the legal education system?

Fogel: I think there's a lot of pressure for a legal education to become more client-centered and interdisciplinary. I believe law schools are trying to deal with how to stay relevant. They're getting feedback not just from the outside community. They're getting it from clients, even corporate clients, who say, "Law students aren't trained to deal with people." They come in knowing how to do legal analysis, but they don't know how to anchor that analysis in real life. They don't understand what's motivating people to come into a law office. I think law schools are trying to respond to that.

It's a struggle though. Law has been taught pretty much the same way for a very long time. It requires some innovation. Before I left for Washington, I taught a seminar at Stanford about that subject. But I think that even at that time the school was becoming more tuned in. Just the fact that they wanted me to teach the seminar is indicative of it.

Bloch: Do you think that's reflected in the admissions process?

Fogel: That I really couldn't say. I think there's a trend toward older students. It reflects a preference for people a little more seasoned—people who have had the chance to explore different alternatives and are consciously choosing law school, rather than just saying, "Well, I got my bachelor's degree, so now I'm moving on to the next step."

I think that this trend in general is a good thing. People now have more life experience to bring to the training.

Law school is a professional school. It's not like the liberal education that you get through high school and in college. It's much more focused. I think that it's something you really have had to have thought through and know that you want to do. If it's the path of least resistance, take some time, get to know yourself better, like what motivates you and what you really care about.

Bloch: Looking back, do you feel like you made the right decision? Would you go back and change anything about the process that you took?

Fogel: When I went to law school, I don't believe that it was a fully formed decision. It was, to some extent, the path of least resistance than some other things I might have done. I know I didn't want to go into academia. I didn't have any other professional intentions at that point either. For me, it was the best alternative, but it wasn't really consciously formed.

Now, it worked out well. I'm not sorry I did it. The thing I would say is that the law is big enough so that you can always find a way to express and be yourself within it. I found my way, and I took a very unconventional path.

When I got out of law school I essentially did legal services work with a population that has not been traditionally represented. I did it because I had a sense that there was a group of people not being served, that needed to be served, and I had a background and interest in that field, so I could serve them.

It's hardly a conventional path to a judgeship, but the great thing about the law is that it allows for you to do these types of things. There's no lockstep that you have to go in.

As students graduate, law schools are often criticized for channeling everyone into big law firms. I think that happens more often than it should, but if you look out five or ten years, you see what people are doing and people really do try and find a way to make it work for themselves. It's a field big enough for that. It has been very good to me and I feel fortunate for how things have worked out.

Bloch: What are you doing now?

Fogel: As you know, I started as a judge on the Santa Clara County Municipal Court in 1981. I spent five years there, then in 1986 moved to the Superior Court. In '98, I moved to the federal district court. I left there last October to become Director of the Federal Judicial Center.

Bloch: Why did you decide to become the Director of the FJC?

Fogel: As of last September I'd judged for 30 years, and I'd done the whole gamut of things judges do. I am really interested in judicial education—how judges are trained and how they can improve their performance. So this was a great opportunity that came along and a number of people who know me well encouraged me to do it. It combined this experience I have as a judge and as a teacher with this larger academic interest that I have in the profession.

So, the opening came along at a time when I was interested in taking on something new, and my background seemed to be a good fit with what the Board was looking for. It's exciting to be here, on a personal level.

Bloch: What final advice would you give to a student like me who's trying to figure out if law school is the right choice?

Fogel: Be sure that it's what you want to do. Know that you want to do it. More importantly, know *why* you want to do it. I don't think it's mandatory to take time off and do something else, but if you're going because you just don't really know what else to do, my advice would be to take a couple years off.

Go and work in some type of job in the non-profit sector or the private sector. Just go see what else is out there. That way, if your interest persists, you can come at it with a different perspective.

Interview V
THE DEPUTY SECRETARY

Kenneth W. Dam

Kenneth Dam has devoted his career to public policy issues, both as a practitioner and a professor. He has served as the Deputy Secretary of State from 1982-1985, Corporate Vice President of IBM from 1985-1992, interim CEO & President of The United Way of America in 1992, and the Deputy Secretary of Treasury from 2001-2003. He is a graduate of the University of Kansas (1954), and received his Juris Doctor degree from the University of Chicago Law School (1957). He is currently a senior fellow of the Brookings Institution, and a professor emeritus and senior lecturer at the University of Chicago Law School.

Bloch: Would you tell me about your childhood?

Dam: I was born and grew up on a farm in Kansas during the Great Depression. I remember vaguely that until I was three-years-old we had no electricity and no running water. We got electricity when Franklin D. Roosevelt implemented his Rural Electrification Program. Then we were able to install a pump in our well instead of having to lift water up by a hand crank. [My upbringing] certainly had an influence on me.

Bloch: And what did your parents do?

Dam: My father was a farmer and an entrepreneur. Starting when I was three- or four-years-old he ran a hatchery. That was a period in which there was a big sickness among chickens and we found a place within the United States where the sickness did not occur, so we bought eggs from there and hatched them in our own hatchery. We had two big incubators. We had a lot of chickens, and we sold baby chicks.

Bloch: Where did you go after the farm?

Dam: I went to high school five miles away in the local town. From there I went to the University of Kansas, where I studied economics. The department was located in the business school so I learned accounting as well. Accounting was one of the best courses I ever took, and it is a very valuable skill for a lawyer.

Bloch: When did you gain an interest in the law?

Dam: From my earliest time, my father had always said I should go to law school. He started college, but couldn't complete it because he had scarlet fever. The biggest regret of his life was that he couldn't get a college education. He was very strong on the fact that I should study law. It was preordained.

Bloch: How would you summarize your law school experience?

Dam: Law school was a very broad-based education for me because of the way law was taught, particularly at that time at the University of Chicago. It was influenced by the liberal arts. The faculty was basically a product of the 30's and 40's when I was going there in the 1950's, so I learned a lot of economics, social and political history, and so forth. I would not have acquired that otherwise.

Also, it was a small law school, and still is, so there was a lot of interaction with the faculty. I knew all the faculty personally, partly through a quirk in that during my third year, there was a boycott by them of the Faculty Club. Because of that, I had lunch with them in the Commons almost every day. I got to know them very well.

Bloch: Would you say that that was the biggest value of your law school experience?

Dam: No, I'd say the biggest value of my law school experience was learning how to work hard, because you really had to.

Also, learning how to write well. Before law school, I wrote well in a journalistic sense. In law school, I learned how to do really careful writing for briefs and scholarly articles.

Bloch: Did that aspect of going to law school help you most in your career?

Dam: I think it was a good background for public affairs. It was particularly good for my law career. I was a good brief writer. I spent a lot of time writing memos that were designed to be converted into briefs after the theory was developed.

Bloch: After you finished law school, what was your career path like?

Dam: I happened to be lucky to get a Supreme Court clerkship right out of law school. I had excellent grades, but I have to admit that it didn't hurt that I was from Kansas. A justice on the Supreme Court named Charles Whittaker happened to be born there. He was a hardworking Court of Appeals judge, but we don't remember him because he served only five years before becoming ill and retiring. I think he thought he'd be more comfortable with a clerk who was from Kansas. He thought I would be someone he could get along with. Of course he had to meet me; it was a one-hour interview and he hired me on the spot.

Bloch: What happened after your clerkship?

Dam: I went to New York and worked for a first-rate law firm called Cravath, Swaine & Moore. It was one of the best law firms in New York, and still is today.

I didn't have a great experience from the standpoint of becoming a partner because I left after only two years due to an idiosyncratic experience with the particular partner I was assigned to. However, while I was there, I became a favorite of the General Counsel of CBS

Television. I spent a lot of time talking to the GC about antitrust law, which piqued my interest in that.

I also did some work for a German firm and for an American firm on a contract in Turkey. I didn't go to Germany or Turkey, but my work in that realm sparked my interest in Western Europe because at the time, Western Europe was like the China of today. It's where everyone wanted to invest and do business.

Bloch: What did you do after your work at the law firm?

Dam: I taught at the University of Chicago for the next 11 years before going to Washington.

Let me explain my international interest. In 1933, a man named Max Rheinstein was working as a comparative law scholar in Germany. He was a German-Jew, so after Hitler took over, he fled for the United States and ended up in Chicago as one of my professors.

I wasn't particularly close to him as a student, but when I began to teach, we became close colleagues. He taught a very intensive course in German and French law for graduate students who would spend their second year in law school abroad in one of those countries. I sat in on that course, which led me to visit both France and Germany in '65 and '66 with my wife, a foreign language enthusiast.

I got an appointment at the university in Freiburg, where I taught some courses but spent a majority of my time learning German law. I was tutored in the subject by assistant professors who used original German texts to instruct me. I had to be proficient in the language in order to solve their law problems. It was pretty intense.

I tried to do the same thing in France, but it didn't work because you just couldn't have the same relationship with French law professors. They didn't have offices at the law school, but rather, I had to travel to their homes in Paris. I still learned a lot of French law, and I learned to speak French better and appreciate French culture.

Bloch: What brought you to Washington?

Dam: The dean of the business school in Chicago, George Shultz, became head of the Office of Management and Budget of the U.S. government. In the U.S., debt, taxation, and budgeting are split up between different departments. The spending function of the Treasury was put in the Executive Office of the President, which today, is the Office of Management and Budget.

I first met Shultz while teaching at Chicago. One day, I said to the law school dean, "We ought to have a joint degree in law and business because some of the courses are available in both schools." He agreed, and sent me to pitch the idea to Shultz.

I remember we met in a room at the Faculty Club. I was on one end of the table, and Shultz and two of his assistant deans were on the other. I negotiated right then and there, which I think really impressed him. I got to know him and many other people on the business school faculty. Since he knew that I was interested in understanding the practice of budgeting, not just the legal theory behind it, he asked me, "Why don't you come and replace Jim Schlesinger?" Schlesinger was the former OMB assistant director who was leaving for another position. I was catapulted immediately to the job of the assistant director responsible for the foreign aid, State Department, and intelligence community budgets.

Bloch: How did the skills you learned in law school and your international experiences help in your position at the Office of Management and Budget?

Dam: I think being in law school and being a law school professor makes you a quick learner. You have to master so much diverse information; you learn what are the issues, what's important, and how to talk and write about things in an intelligent way. More than just the law, that's what law school is all about.

Bloch: What did you do after your position at the Office of Management and Budget?

Dam: I made a small transition along with Shultz, who was named Secretary of Treasury for the Nixon administration. Nixon didn't like the idea of having to deal with all these competing departments. He wanted to coordinate economic policy in one place, so he put [Henry] Kissinger in charge of foreign policy and Shultz in charge of economic policy. He tried to do it in other areas, but it just didn't gel.

So I was promoted to Executive Director of the White House Council on Economic Policy. I had an office in the West Wing. I was able to work up policy choices and do the basic work so that decisions could be made on different initiatives, like welfare reform.

I had to go back to Chicago to keep my tenure position, but I was anxious to get out anyways because Nixon was like a fort under siege at the White House. He ultimately resigned in '74, about four or five months after I left.

Bloch: How many more years did you stay at Chicago for?

Dam: I stayed until 1981 until I got a call from Shultz to be his deputy in the State Department for the Reagan administration. He had just been appointed Secretary of State to replace Alexander Haig, who had flamed out and had to resign from the position. So I was the number two in the State Department for almost three years.

Bloch: What's the main difference between the work Shultz did as Secretary of State and what you did as his deputy?

Dam: Mine was more a management role. I remember that day in October when I was sworn in to the position. I took the oath at 7 a.m., and Shultz left on the 8 a.m. plane for the United Nations, where the Secretary of State has to be every year during that month when the General Assembly meets. I didn't hear from him for almost a month. But, this was a serious time—the marines were in Lebanon—and I had a lot of day-to-day responsibility. I had to receive heads of government, for example. It was a lot of fast learning about diplomacy.

I remember when I needed an executive assistant. I said to the people in the State Department, "Look, I know a lot about the world, but I don't know anything about the Middle East. That's the half I never learned anything about." And they chose Edward Walker, who later became Ambassador to the United Arab Emirates, Egypt, and Israel. He practically lived with me because he knew all the issues and all the people. It shows that the State Department is well organized and always has been in modern times. I had a lot of good coaching.

Bloch: Then you went to IBM. Can you tell me about that transition?

Dam: I had an offer to be an officer of the company in charge of worldwide government relations, intellectual property, and some other functions.

The initial plan was for me to be General Counsel, but the CEO and I both recognized that that plan would not have worked, so I got a whole lot of other assignments instead. I was in charge of things like export controls, the US education program—moving on-site education in Atlanta to electronic education—and our giving program. Although IBM doesn't have an official charitable foundation, because of its history it was giving away as much money as the Ford Foundation at the time. I was running that, although my primary job was to cut that budget because IBM wasn't doing well at that point. Even though they invented the laptop, they were not making the transition to the laptop era very well. After a while, it began to hurt earnings, so I had to cut the charitable budget substantially. Either way it was still a good experience.

Bloch: And after that you became President and CEO of United Way?

Dam: I planned on retiring from IBM at 60—the mandatory retirement age—and since I going to be leaving soon anyways, John Akers, who was both the CEO of IBM and Chairman of the Board at United Way, figured he'd accelerate that and let me take the United Way job.

There was a scandal there involving a man named William Aramony. I really just had to clean up his mess. United Way had all kinds of problems with fraud and financial mismanagement, so I traveled all over the country explaining to volunteers what happened and getting rid of the loopholes that allowed Aramony to commit fraud. I also had to find a new CEO, who ended up being Elaine Chao. She later became Secretary of Labor.

Bloch: What was it like trying to clean up the mess?

Dam: We had a very strong Board at the United Way, which helped. We had Bill Gates and the CEO of IBM on the board. As a matter of fact, I introduced Bill to John Akers. They had never met at that point. It was at a dinner, and I thought they ought to meet. I was sitting next to Mrs. Gates, Melinda, and I found out they had never met John, so I walked over to Akers and said, "I think you two ought to meet."

Bloch: It's amazing all the connections a person in your standing gains over the years. What do you think got you to this point?

Dam: I've been very fortunate that way. I'm on the Board of the Council on Foreign Relations in New York too, which is the old Eastern establishment. It's a series of quirks based on two things, if I may summarize: human relations—getting along with people—and, doing the work. Human relations gets you nowhere if you can't do the work.

Bloch: On that note of "doing the work," what's one piece of advice you would give to a student who's looking to go into government or public policy?

Dam: Well you certainly don't have to go to law school. It's a good background, but it's not necessary. No matter what, you have to understand that there is no substitute for knowing the issues in-depth, and for that, you have to be able to learn, study, and work. Even though it's important, you can't just go out to lunch with people. There's no substitute for hard work and putting in the time.

I think there's a shallowness to public policy making today, which is regrettable. People think that if they just know the political slogans, that's all that's needed. But, if you're going to reform the welfare system, you need to know about it in great detail.

I'm afraid that modern-day social networking leads to sloganizing. I see it all the time in the press. There are very few articles—even in *The New York Times*—that are really in-depth. For example, there was recently a piece in *The New York Times* about energy. It was one of the best things I've found in a long time. But if you read the daily articles on energy, they're not very helpful. It's not because people can't write like that, but because daily coverage is such that you have to deal with the latest political flap.

Bloch: What's the best way to fix that?

Dam: Get better people in government. And, I think it's partly a media problem.

In my view, the media started going downhill when television news was no longer centered around the evening news broadcasts on CBS, NBC, and ABC. It became a 24-hour news cycle. At that point, 24-hour reporting had to be superficial. They don't have time to do analysis; they rush it out immediately with a summary. That led to all the other substitutes for the formal media that we have now. This is a dumbing down of public policy analysis, in my opinion.

Bloch: Would you say that need for better people in government is what motivated you to go back to the Treasury Department in the early 2000's?

Dam: No, not particularly. I just got the opportunity to go and I was interested in the issues. I got a call from the Secretary of the Treasury, Paul O'Neill, with whom I had been at the Office of Management and Budget and on the Board at Alcoa when he was the Chairman and CEO. He knew me very well; I guess he thought he could work well with me and asked me to be deputy.

You just don't turn down jobs like that. I'm not claiming it's a great desire for public service—I like being in government—but I wouldn't say I was idealistic in taking the job. I just thought it was a great opportunity both to serve and to learn.

Bloch: With the wide range of experiences that you've had including academia, the public sector, and the private sector, which is your

favorite?

Dam: I like the public sector the most because I feel like I've done the most, and am able to do the most, there. I still do things that are related to the public sector. I've been on advisory committees and so forth, and although I don't write that much anymore, when I do, I write about public sector issues.

Bloch: Would you change anything about your career path?

Dam: No, I don't think so. I haven't really looked at it that way. You do what you do. I sit on a lot of non-profit boards, and I got a lot of satisfaction from giving back. For example, I'm on the Board of the Brookings Institution and I work a lot with the American Enterprise Institute, which houses the Shadow Financial Regulatory Committee. I'm with the Chicago Council on Global Affairs. I enjoy doing those kind of things, and I think it's public service in another way. I do believe in public service. People with skills and experience are badly needed in both public affairs and public service.

Bloch: What is it like being involved with the Brookings Institution?

Dam: There are a lot of good people there. I go to the Board meetings because I'm an honorary trustee and an adjunct scholar. We hear a lot of very good scholars discuss issues, from Pakistan to welfare reform to immigration, and so forth. Also, there are very interesting board members who you get to know. The next board meeting involves our international advisory board and there will be people there from Europe, India, Japan, and more. My wife enjoys attending the meetings as well. It's a family activity to a certain extent.

Bloch: What is one piece of advice you would give to a student who's thinking about going into law?

Dam: Study and get good grades. Work hard. I studied every night until midnight preparing for the next day's classes. It was good training because it meant that when I needed to do something I could sit down and do it. You have to have that foundation for people to take you seriously.

You also need to learn the issues. The issues are complicated. The level of "the Twitter discussion" is not where reform or progress is made in public policy. If you go to law school and are interested in public policy, you need to take the courses that are applicable to public policy.

You need to learn all the basics; you need to learn procedure particularly, so you can understand the cases. But at the end of the day, take the public law courses because they're good background if you want to go into public policy.

Interview VI
THE PARTNER

Jonathan K. Layne

Jonathan Layne is a partner at Gibson, Dunn & Crutcher's Century City office, where he co-chairs the Firm's Mergers & Acquisitions Group and is a member of the Firm's Executive Committee. He graduated from The College of William & Mary (1975) and received a joint JD/MBA from Emory University (1979), where he was a member of the Order of the Coif and was the Managing Editor of the Law Journal. Layne has been selected by "Chambers and Partners" as a Leading Mergers and Acquisitions lawyer each year since 2005, and as a Leading Capital Markets: Debt & Equity lawyer each year since 2007. He is a member of both the Business Law Sections of the American Bar Association and the State Bar of California.

Bloch: Could you tell me a little bit about your time growing up?

Layne: I grew up outside of New York City and for college, I went to The College of William & Mary, where I majored in Economics. After that, I received my JD/MBA at Emory University in Atlanta.

Bloch: Where did your interest in law and business first begin?

Layne: It probably started with business first, then law. I think it started at the dinner table, because my dad was in the brokerage business.

Bloch: Did you ever want to go into brokerage like your father?

Layne: I never had that desire. But I did always have an orientation toward business and business issues. He would come home every night with *The Wall Street Journal*, and he had *BusinessWeek* on the coffee table. We would often have business conversations at dinner. I suppose living in that environment developed my interest in business, particularly entrepreneurship and watching people raise capital, deploy capital, and grow companies.

Bloch: Why did you decide to get a law degree if business was always your interest?

Layne: I applied to a couple of programs and went to business school first. I almost went to the Darden School of Business at the University of Virginia, but Emory wrote me a big check! Back then, there weren't loans as much as graduate assistantships and fellowships. From time-to-time they would find students that they really wanted and then give them money. So I was drawn down there and started business school. Often the JD/MBA program will start with law school then business school, but I didn't do that. I went to business school first.

Bloch: Is that something unique to Emory?

Layne: I don't think so. I wouldn't say it's unique, but most of the time people go to law school first. They'll spend their first year in law school, second year in business school, and then the last two years as a mixture. I did business school first, then my first year of law school, and in my last two years I did both.

Bloch: How would you characterize your law school experience?

Layne: It was quite positive. I liked my law school. It's a different analytical process than in business school. I loved business school too; I had great experiences with professors and classmates, but it's quite different than law school.

Bloch: What was the biggest difference between them?

Layne: The way you're taught to think. The way you approach problems. Business school back then was about 50/50 between text and case. The first year of business school is probably 75% text, essentially learning business principles. Then, the second part of your first year you start getting into cases, and later on, cases become more important and text less so.

Law school is almost 100% case. It's a different approach. You're reading cases instead of black letters. You're learning how to extract principles out of cases instead of being spoon-fed principles.

Bloch: Which did you enjoy more?

Layne: I enjoyed case. Once I had some core principles under my belt, I enjoyed them more. I don't think learning business straight out of the case is the most efficient approach. I think there's a value in having a certain amount of text delivered to you in concentrated form, which from there, you can develop and see how relevant it is to the case mechanism. Different schools have different processes. Harvard Business School has always been very case-oriented, and Wharton is a little bit more text-oriented.

Bloch: What would you say was the toughest part of your graduate school experience?

Layne: I think the toughest part was probably the first semester of law school. It's a huge adjustment in your process of thinking. There's an unnecessary amount of nonsense that goes on, so you have to filter your way through it. It probably adds to the stress level more than it ever should.

Other than that I can't think of any part of it that was really difficult. A warning though: it's a long haul. Four years is a long time, and for me particularly since I went straight through to my JD/MBA after my undergraduate studies, it's a lot of schooling.

Bloch: If you could go back, would you still go directly into the JD/MBA program?

Layne: I don't think there are any major decisions I would change. I thought for a while as to whether I should take time off between college and law school, but I think it was the right decision for me.

Back then business schools were willing to accept students right out of college. That's changed, although there are some exceptions. I think the average age of MBA students nowadays is closer to 26-years-old than it is to 22-years-old.

Bloch: What was the biggest value of your graduate studies?

Layne: I was taught to think quickly and decisively about how to solve complex issues which require a multi-disciplinary approach. It's rare to bring a comprehensive set of skills to the marketplace, particularly if you're interested in business law. Having a strong accounting and finance background is very important. I think it's a differentiator. Also, I found that having marketing expertise is helpful to understanding marketing theories and practices. I would say corporate law, accounting, finance, and marketing are probably the four skill sets that I found most useful.

I think you can really pick up a much better understanding of the business world if you have a law degree, and a much better understanding of the legal world if you have a business degree. I see it every day in my practice. Junior lawyers who have no financial background and who are trying to practice in the corporate area are at a disadvantage. I am a big believer in people understanding how to read balance sheets and income statements. So I tell them to immediately go out and take some accounting classes and finance courses.

Bloch: Why did you decide to go to Gibson, Dunn & Crutcher after graduation?

Layne: I interviewed with law firms in seven cities and I was fortunate to receive offers from firms in all seven. I came to Gibson Dunn because I liked the people and I saw entrepreneurial spirit with a great opportunity for growth.

I started with Gibson Dunn when we had 185 lawyers in four offices (all in the U.S. plus Paris) and now we have 1,100 lawyers in 17 offices around the world. I knew that they were going to roll out an international platform, and I wanted to be a part of the growth and excitement. I just really liked the people and culture.

Bloch: What practice do you focus on at Gibson Dunn?

Layne: I co-head our global Mergers & Acquisitions efforts, so I spend most of my time these days on that. Our work covers representing public companies, private companies, and private equity groups in change of control, joint venture, and investment transactions around the world.

Bloch: Why did you decide to hone in on M&A?

Layne: I've done it all through the years—capital markets, private equity, securities law, corporate governance. I find M&A work to be interesting and collaborative. We're constantly working with smart people from top-tier companies and investment banks toward a common goal.

Bloch: What is one piece of advice you would give a student who is thinking about getting a JD/MBA and going into business law?

Layne: My advice is to sit down and think about what you're really looking to achieve. What are your strengths and weaknesses? Is this something you are really attracted to? Know what it is you find rewarding and intellectually stimulating and know whether this is an area in which you will likely reach your personal growth potential.

Those questions are difficult to answer but you have to understand what's involved in the path and whether that's something you will really enjoy. Much of this is conjecture on your part but you should be able to assess a good portion of it if you are honest with yourself. If you do not know exactly what type of business law you want to go into (i.e. M&A, securities, capital markets, bankruptcy, etc.), that's okay. You do not need to make up your mind this early. It's certainly fine not to know now although I do find that people who have a better idea early on tend to progress faster because they are more focused.

The four-year JD/MBA program is a long haul and it's not inexpensive, particularly when you factor in opportunity costs. You should try to consider what type of return you are likely to receive for your investment.

Interview VII
THE SCREENWRITER

Roger S. Wolfson

Roger Wolfson is a television and film writer who currently serves as a writer and producer for the USA TV series *Fairly Legal*. He has written for many television programs, including *Law & Order: Special Victims Unit*, *Saving Grace*, *The Closer*, and *Century City*. He is a graduate of Vassar College, received his Master of Arts in Creative Writing from Johns Hopkins University, and received his Juris Doctor degree from the University of Pennsylvania Law School, where he was Associate Editor of the Comparative Labor Law Journal. Before becoming a writer, he served as committee staff member for Senator Joe Lieberman, speechwriter for Senator John Kerry, Chief Education Counsel for Senator Paul Wellstone, and committee staff member for Senator Edward Kennedy.

Bloch: Where are you from?

Wolfson: I grew up in New Haven, Connecticut. My father is a Professor of Cardiology at Yale. I was raised in a very educational environment and went to Jewish day school. My carpool driver was Joe Lieberman. Always had to be an American car! He was my mother's law partner and my best friend's father. I spent almost as much time with Joe growing up as I did with my own family.

I attended Vassar College as a drama major before going to the University of Pennsylvania Law School. After I graduated, I practiced civil rights law in New Haven for less than a year. I became counsel for Joe Lieberman, then John Kerry's speechwriter, and later chief education counsel for Ted Kennedy and Paul Wellstone.

Bloch: How did your interest in law first begin?

Wolfson: My parents largely. Although they believed in me and my acting abilities, they weren't especially encouraging about the idea of going into a creative profession. Not because they didn't believe in me, but they didn't trust the creative atmosphere. They strongly encouraged me to go to some form of graduate school, so I got the law degree with the idea that I was just going to get the degree to fall back on, and then go to be an actor anyway.

After I started practicing law, I really felt like it was a golden opportunity to *write* law, because it really was an exciting time for politics. Clinton was in office, and the Democrats had a majority in both the Senate and the House. Even while I was working in politics, as much as I loved it and it was highly rewarding, it wasn't creatively satisfying. I actually earned my master's degree in creative writing while working in Senate.

Bloch: Where did you earn your master's degree?

Wolfson: Johns Hopkins. They had a Washington D.C. branch in Dupont Circle so I was able to go there part-time while working in Senate.

Bloch: Even though your parents pushed you to go to law school, it's great that you pursued your own interests simultaneously.

Wolfson: It's quite remarkable. As it happens, all my experiences kind of set on each other. Even though now I'm a full-time writer, and I have been for nine years, I'm still very politically active. I've been very involved with my former professor Elizabeth Warren's Senate campaign.

I've been involved in the Governor's race [California], the Gore/Lieberman campaign, the Kerry/Edwards campaign, and I expect I'll probably be somewhat involved in the 2012 presidential election as well. I do that now for fun, just to keep my political muscles toned. Even though my career is no longer based on it, it's rewarding to stay involved in politics.

Bloch: How would you describe your law school experience?

Wolfson: Law school is very challenging. My view is that up until about 40 or 50 years ago, you didn't even have to go to law school to practice law. You just had to apprentice as a lawyer and then pass the bar. I think law schools are self-generating, self-funding mechanisms. When law schools first started they were bachelors' degrees, they weren't even doctorates. I still feel as though law school is designed to drag itself out. I don't know that people get well trained in law school as lawyers. Law school has just become a form of business. I keyed into that early on and I was a little bit resentful of it.

However, I went to Penn, and it's more than just a law school—it's actually the first university in the nation. While everything else was a college, Penn was designed to be a university. I had friends at Wharton, I had friends at the architecture school, I had friends all over different departments at Penn, and it was really at law school that I learned how to live life. I used to go to arboretums and museums every weekend, and I read a lot of books. I started the practice of reading a book a week while I was in law school. I really ended up making the most of my experiences. I volunteered at different organizations. I got really into movies. I really feel law school was the beginning of my life as an adult.

Bloch: Would you say that was the biggest value of going to law school?

Wolfson: Yes. It was sort of the transition between childhood and adulthood for me. My professional awakening was in the halls of the Senate and on the Senate floor. In the seven years I worked at the Senate, I had one of the most incredible experiences someone could have had. I worked for four of the most prominent members of my party—a diverse group, and all of them presidential candidates at one time or another. All of them real leaders in their own rights. I wouldn't have had that experience if it wasn't for law school.

By the same token, I've written for five TV shows and I've written four pilots, so I'm successful, but for almost all the shows I've worked on the law degree has helped me get the job. Half of my pilots have had some form of legal content, based off my legal experience. In the world of writing, if you have a law degree you're always considered to be apt and prepared for a cop or detective show, not just law shows.

Bloch: How would you say law school has helped you, if at all, in both your careers—in the Senate and as a writer?

Wolfson: Law school has helped me with everything I've done. There was a third and a fourth career in there as well; I was basically Vice President for two years of a television news company called Channel One. I have also run a political consulting firm.

A law degree helped me with all of that. It communicates loud and clear: I'm a brand in my own right. I'm an established professional. I have skills. I have weight.

In the work force, before you get any job, you have to have confidence in yourself. You have to believe you're worth whatever amount of money they are offering to pay you. You have to believe that you have something to offer. A law degree is incredibly helpful because it gives you that level of confidence. And it is also one of the more empowering potential degrees because you basically have a license to stand up for yourself and for others. It's a powerful degree.

Bloch: Looking back, would you get that law degree again if you could relive the decision, or do you think you could be as successful as you are now without that experience?

Wolfson: It's impossible to say. What I can tell you is that I'm deeply grateful for the law degree. The thought of going back through it is not a pleasant one, because law school was so intense. I would certainly want to try the experience of just writing without ever having gotten my degree, but all the opportunities it allowed me changed how I look at the world. It gave me a perspective that makes me believe that I have more to say, and more *important* things to say, than I ever could have if I had never gone to law school.

Bloch: Can you tell me more about how you became a screenwriter?

Wolfson: In 2002, I was living on a sailboat—sailing up and down the coast of the United States—running my political consulting firm. I had about 40 people working for me, most people working from home while my best friend and I were working from the deck of the boat and running the firm through use of our cell phones. Right around that time Paul Wellstone was killed in an airplane crash. Someone I hired while I was working for him was on the plane. One of my partners, Marilyn Haft, former Deputy Counsel for Vice President Walter Mondale, and former U.S. Representative to the United Nations, pointed out to me that I could have been on that plane with Paul. She said to me, "If you had died on that plane, people would have been able to say that you loved what you were doing, but no one would be able to say that you were doing what you loved to do. You can't wait any longer. You can't wait. If you want to be a writer, you have to do it."

Life is short. It was very easy to accept that with Paul recently having died, but setting sail for Los Angeles was another thing altogether. I had to convince my other partners to buy into it. I had to convince my friends to help me sail it. I had to convince my family to support me, at least emotionally, and I had to give up on this pretty big successful career that I had. I decided to sail down through the Panama Canal, and in March of '03, I arrived in Los Angeles. Within a month, I was represented by CAA [Creative Artists Agency], and two months later I was writing for a TV show. It usually doesn't happen that fast. I know some people who had pretty amazing success stories like that, but not many.

Bloch: To what do you attribute the speed of your success upon arriving in LA?

Wolfson: The real key was back when I worked for Channel One. Andy Hill, the producer, and I became very good friends. He was formerly the President of CBS Productions, the studio for CBS. When I moved to LA, I asked him to make some introductions, and he set me up with a guy named Larry Lyttle. He was a producer for Big Ticket Television, which makes TV shows like Judge Judy. On Andy's request, Larry took me out to lunch. At the end of the lunch, I heard what every writer would dream of hearing. This guy ran a studio, he used to help run Warner Brothers Television, and he said to me after our lunch, "Kid, I like you. I'm going to launch you."

I said to him, "Larry, I like you too. I'm going to launch you."

We each made a phone call for each other. He called the agent at CAA who ended up representing me, and I called Joe Lieberman.

Within a matter of months I was represented and writing professionally. And he, believe it or not, had quit Paramount and Big Ticket Television to work on Joe Lieberman's presidential race as his media consultant.

In the course of one lunch we profoundly changed each other's careers. In fact, he went toward my old career as I went toward his. We've been friends ever since.

Bloch: Was it easier to find success once the right introductions were made?

Wolfson: Just getting a meeting with an agent wasn't enough. I had to prove that I could write, and I did. The CAA met with me. They said, "You seem like a nice guy, and you can be the nicest guy in the world, but unless you can write, we can't get you staffed." So I asked them what they wanted to see from me. They wanted a West Wing.

Over the next three weeks I worked on a script, and at the end, that script got me offers of representation not just from CAA, but from other agencies as well.

That was in the hiring season of '03, and I had just written the West Wing, but it wasn't enough to demonstrate that I had scope or range. So my agent said, "If you really want to get staffed this year, you have to write a crime show. You have to write *The Shield*." And I said, "What's *The Shield*?" They sent me home with all 24 episodes of the show, and I came back to the office with a really great show spec two weeks to the day that they told me what the show was. And at that point, the CAA completely believed in me. I had proven myself to them.

My first TV writing job was on *Century City*, about a law firm 25 years in the future. The writers on that staff went on to create *House*. Before I could even end up on *House*, which I like to think they would have brought me on board for, I was already writing for *Law and Order: SVU*. After that I wrote for *The Closer*. I wrote an episode that got Kyra Sedgwick nominated for an Emmy Award, and since then I've been able to sell shows on my own. I wrote for *Saving Grace* and *Fairly Legal*. Right now I have a blind script deal at ABC that I'm working on. I haven't decided what it's going to be yet. They have to be involved in it; they'll be involved every step of the way.

Bloch: What do you feel the future holds for you in your screenwriting career? What do you hope to accomplish in the next few years?

Wolfson: I want to get my own show on the air. It could be anything. I have a couple of shows that I'm working on about sailing, law, presidential politics, even NASA! I have a lot of really different ideas. It's fun. It's exciting.

Now I have more experience as a professional writer than anything else I've ever done. I know what I'm doing, I know how to come up with ideas, I know how to write. That's not saying that I'm not still growing as an artist, because I am, and it's not to say that I'm not growing as a person either, because I am immensely.

One thing I'm very grateful for is that so far for my entire professional career I've been involved in such competitive industries, at such a high level, that it's really forced me to grow up and to be my best self. I'm not saying I'm there yet, but all of these careers have challenged me to the utmost.

Bloch: Given that lesson and the wide range of experiences that you have, what is one piece of advice you would give to an undergraduate student who is thinking about becoming a screenwriter?

Wolfson: Work hard. I mean it. Really, really work hard.

Writers are some of the most brilliant and confident people that I've ever met. It's amazing. When you're the head of a show, you have 300 people working for you, full-time, like an orchestra. Talented people, doing very interesting things, at the very, very best of their abilities. Every one of them have trained their entire lives to do this and they're completely at the disposal of the show runner to accentuate his or her vision. You have to be so incredibly involved to do any of that. People who just show up and say, "Oh, I'll try my hand at this," or "Oh, I've only read two or three scripts but I'll bet I can do this"—those people offend me. They think they can not learn the craft or that they can not give it their best and still get paid. Because, you know something, those people are never going to make it. And, it's just disrespectful.

I'm in awe of the size and scope of the television audience. I'm honored that the very first TV episode I wrote was watched by more people than ever heard any speech I ever previously wrote. Even when I wrote for Ted Kennedy! I think anybody who approaches this field should feel honored as well. So, work hard. We read thousands of scripts. If the professional readers in this town—the ones you're going to try to sell to—have read thousands, you should too.

It's an incredibly competitive industry. You've got to read, you've got to learn, you've got to delve into this, you've got to study this, you've got to put your best foot forward. If you really *want* to throw yourself into it, then you know it's the right industry for you. Look at me—I gave up a good career to try my hand at this. I moved out here—I *sailed* out here—I literally moved my whole home in an irreversible way. I came here and I threw myself into it with everything I had and it worked out for me. But it working out for me has required a tremendous amount of discipline and study. When people tell me they want to be a writer, but they don't want to move to Los Angeles, all I can say is good luck.

Some people have said they want to be screenwriters, but they think they can just write a script without having studied it? I'm not saying you have to go to school for it. I have a master's degree in Creative Writing, but they didn't teach me screenwriting. I studied it myself. Before I wrote my episode of *The West Wing* I read at least 50 Aaron Sorkin episodes of *The West Wing*. I diagrammed them like they were legal papers. I broke them down. I figured out everything I could that was formulaic. I studied how he wrote his lines and how long each one of his scenes were. Most TV shows have an A plot and B plot, but *The West Wing* has A, B, C, D, E, and F plots. I studied that. When I finished my version you could lay my script next to an Aaron Sorkin draft, and they would look similar. I'm not saying I'm as good as Aaron Sorkin—that would be hubris to the highest order—but if you laid my script down next to a West Wing you would have to work hard to figure out where I might have missed something. That's what I tell people if they want to write screenplays.

Bloch: I must say that after everything you just said, I feel very naïve. I don't think I ever truly understood the amount of work and effort that goes into being a successful screenwriter.

Wolfson: If you really want to learn about screenwriting, Google a conversation between Steven Spielberg, George Lucas, and Lawrence Kasdan. You'll see three geniuses. You'll see how they came up with *Raiders of the Lost Ark*. You'll see what their thought process was, what their roles were, how furiously they picked the subject matter, and how much effort and thought and understanding went into it. It's beautiful. It's gorgeous. Of course, the movie was a work of art, an unbelievable work of art, but it didn't get that way accidently. It was filled with great intention and skill and heart.

They threw themselves into it aggressively, with everything they had. Look what James Cameron did to get *Avatar* in the air. They say he's maniacal; they say he drives people aggressively. I have no doubt that he drives himself most aggressively of all. As a result, he gives us works of abiding beauty and power.

Bloch: Would you say that your ambition and passion toward perfection in screenwriting comes from the same place as the successes you saw in Senate?

Wolfson: Absolutely. Paul Wellstone was probably the greatest man I've ever known. I've never met anybody so committed, so passionate, so self-effacing, so honest, and so helpful. Paul would be in the office, and when the receptionist wasn't there, he'd answer phone calls simply saying, "Hi, this is Paul." He wouldn't say he's a Senator. Whenever he went to some big fancy hotel he'd walk into the kitchen and first say hello to the people in there. He knew that if he went to those events and didn't stop at the kitchen, he would end up becoming like those people at those big fancy events. He was going to lose touch. He was determined to never lose touch, and he never did.

All the professions I've been in, the temptation to stop being human is massive. If you're a successful screenwriter, no one treats you like a human. If you're a successful Senator, no one treats you like a human. They fawn over you, so staying real is a challenge. Paul worked incredibly hard and was incredibly committed. That's not taking anything away from Kennedy, Kerry, or Lieberman. I could speak just as much, and just as positively, about all three of them. In fact, don't get me started.

Bloch: What is one piece of advice you would give to someone who's thinking about going into law in general?

Wolfson: I would recommend that people who really want to go into law either get a job at a law firm before they go to law school or try shadowing a lawyer for a day or two.

I didn't know anything about what I was getting myself into. I should have done some research first. Going to law school now is an expensive proposition. You have to take out so many loans you may not be able to get out of it. You should try to make sure that you want to practice law before going to law school.

I'd also recommend that which law school you go to is not as important as how much you spend on it. If you want to have any flexibility—if you want to try different careers—you have to avoid debt. It's much better to go to a law school you don't think is quite as good, but emerge as close to no debt as you can, than go to a "better" law school and be forced to spend years practicing law. This is your life you're talking about here.

I would also recommend that in the summer before you go to law school, take the bar review course. Only one friend of mine has ever followed my advice, but he did exceedingly well in law school as a result. The bar review course tells you everything. It's basically all of law school in a summer. It's a couple thousand dollars, but now you'll know all the black letter law. Think how much better you're going to do in law school.

Bloch: I've never heard that before. That's great advice.

Wolfson: I'm the only person I know who gives it. Bar review is frankly more fun that law school too.

Bloch: Do you have any additional advice or anything you'd like to talk about?

Wolfson: One of the smartest things you could do is seek mentors. Learning how to ask for advice and guidance is the smartest thing anyone could do in any profession. If you don't know something, start the process by asking people who do know about it. It's a really smart way to advantage yourself, and it's a very smart way to live.

Interview VIII
THE GOVERNOR

Jennifer M. Granholm

Jennifer Granholm served as the 47th Governor of Michigan (D) from 2003 – 2011. She is a graduate of the University of California, Berkeley (1984), and she received her Juris Doctor degree from Harvard Law School (1987) where she served as the Editor-in-Chief of the Civil Rights-Civil Liberties Law Review. She clerked for U.S. Judge Damon Keith on the Sixth Circuit of the U.S. Court of Appeals, was Michigan's Attorney General from 1999 – 2003, and is now the host of *The War Room with Jennifer Granholm* on Current TV. She is also a Distinguished Practitioner of Law and Public Policy at UC Berkeley's School of Law and Goldman School of Public Policy.

Bloch: Can you take me back to how you grew up?

Granholm: I was born in Canada but moved to California with my parents when I was four-years-old. My dad worked his way up the banking system; he started as a bank teller but ended up becoming president of a bank out here in Northern California.

Both my parents are Republicans. In fact, in high school, I worked for Gerald Ford's campaign trying to get him elected. After high school, I took some time off and went to Los Angeles to become an actress. It was a terrible decision! It was clearly a "try something and if it doesn't work out go to college" decision. In 1980, I also worked on John B. Anderson's presidential campaign. I was inspired by those experiences, and my independent reading of politics and philosophy, to go to UC Berkeley as an undergraduate and major in Political Science and French. Majoring in French was less useful than Political Science, but it did help me while I spent a year in France during my junior year abroad.

Bloch: What did you do after graduating from Berkeley?

Granholm: I got into Harvard Law School. I was the first person in my family to graduate from college, so it was a big deal to go to Harvard. While I was there I was elected to be Editor-in-Chief of the Harvard Civil Rights-Civil Liberties Law Review, since at the time, I wanted to become a civil rights lawyer.

Bloch: What did you do after finishing Harvard Law?

Granholm: I ended up clerking for a judge in Michigan, and later, clerked for Judge Damon Keith on the Sixth Circuit Court of Appeals. He is a big civil rights advocate. It was a huge honor to work with him because he's not just a judge of the Detroit area—he's an icon. He brought us with him to all of his events; we three clerks were almost like his children in tow. Because of him, I got to be introduced to the whole political scene in Michigan.

My husband and I [the two met at Harvard] married in between my second and third year of law school. After graduation, we moved to Detroit proper because we felt our work could have a large impact there. I worked for a county executive. I worked for the judge. I worked full-time on the Dukakis presidential campaign. Ultimately though, I ended up working for the U.S. Attorney's office and did a lot of prosecution work. From there, I ran the Wayne County Corporation Counsel, the largest civil practice of a public firm in the state, to becoming Attorney General and Governor. That was my trajectory.

Bloch: What started your interest in law?

Granholm: I've always been totally enamored with the underdog, and I think a lot of that came from when I was in Los Angeles. While I was a tour guide at Universal Studios, during my breaks I would sit on this little patio and read books about philosophy. After a while, I really felt that Los Angeles was just not the place for me. I felt this burning feeling that I was in the wrong place and not making a difference in the world. I felt a desire to change things, especially for people and places that had no voice. I felt a calling to help them, and I figured law is a great way to do that.

Bloch: How would you describe your law school experience at Harvard?

Granholm: I loved it. It was the best educational experience I have ever had. Up to that point, I had always been in big public schools. Even though it's a huge law school, at Harvard I felt connected. I felt connected to my classes and my section, the grappling of ideas, and the rigors of the curriculum. At Harvard, I've never met so many people who wanted to become President. People who wanted to change the world. People who believed that this mutual platform of education could serve as a launchpad to the presidency.

Bloch: What was the best part your law school experience?

Granholm: I think the best experience was being the Editor-in-Chief of the Civil Rights-Civil Liberties Law Review. It was the largest in number in terms of the law review staffs. If you look at the roster of the CRCL, it had almost 100 students! It was huge, and everybody was so committed to the issue of civil rights. That was definitely a wonderful experience. That was also the first time I'd been elected to anything, so it was quite an honor and a very great experience for me.

Bloch: What was the worst part about being at Harvard Law?

Granholm: I wouldn't call it the worst, but there's one experience that was definitely the most tense. Back in the mid-80's, I was part of a group that was protesting Harvard's business investments in South Africa. [At that time, South Africa was racially segregated under Apartheid]. We did things like camp out in front of Harvard President Derek Bok's house and chant, "Derek Bok, get the word. This is not Johannesburg!"

When the South African ambassador came to speak on campus one day, a few members of the group protested by lying down in front of his vehicle and blocking it from moving forward. I didn't lie down in the street with them, but because I was a part of the group, I was brought in front of the disciplinary board to see whether or not I should be kicked out of school.

For me, coming from a family with very humble roots, it was like, "I'll get kicked out of Harvard for this." But in the end, we were represented in front of the board by one of the law professors who was an esteemed criminal defense lawyer. He got us out of trouble. I ended up getting a note about the incident put in my file, but thankfully I didn't get kicked out.

Bloch: Did that incident launch your interest in politics? When did you first think about running for office?

Granholm: I've always been totally interested in politics and in changing the world, but I never thought of myself as running for office. In fact, my husband, Dan, was the one interested in running for office, and we actually moved back to Michigan to give him a chance to do that. Before we got married, the priest who prepared us asked what we wanted to do when we were older. We told him that Dan wanted to go into politics, and I wanted to change the world by being a civil rights lawyer. The priest asked him, "Well what if the party comes to Jennifer? What if there's an open seat for her?" And Dan said, "I'd support her 100%." And he did.

Bloch: While you were governor, was there any one defining moment that encompassed all the skills that you learned in law school?

Granholm: There's not just one moment, it's all the time. For example, the first month I was in office, Michigan was in the midst of a massive budget crisis. Usually the budget director goes in front of the legislature alone to present the budget. However, to make the case for the cuts that I was proposing, I also went before the legislature. The ability to feel comfortable doing that—negotiating with the legislature, drafting legislation, you name it—emerged on day one on the job and all evolved from my experiences in law school.

Bloch: Looking back, from the clerkship to Attorney General to Governor, how did your law degree help you in your career path?

Granholm: Having a foundation in which people cannot attack your qualifications or your education is of prime importance. Had I not had my credentials from Harvard Law, I likely wouldn't have been approached to run for Attorney General. That unassailable credential is extremely important, especially for a young woman.

Law school gives you the ability to question, to speak truth to power, and to feel comfortable doing the research for your case. Law school's encouragement of Socratic dialogue and thinking through problems is phenomenal training for any path, and certainly great for politics.

When I think of my colleagues at Harvard, Eliot Spitzer for example, it's clear that having people with great analytical minds argue and debate school work with you sets you up ideally in running for office. I debated all the time in law school, and that skill helped me immensely when I was debating an opponent at the next podium or delivering a speech to a crowd. Those skills were honed in my law school training.

Bloch: Why transition into TV?

Granholm: It certainly wasn't something I pursued. The network is partially owned by Al Gore. He called me and said, "We're putting together a primetime lineup, it's a startup network, and we're going to build it out. We want you to host one of the shows." It sounded like fun, so I did it.

Bloch: Do you do the research for the show in addition to hosting it?

Granholm: Since I'm the host I do research on my guests, the questions I'd like to ask them, and the themes I want to focus on. For example, we've been following the story of ALEC, the American Legislative Exchange Council. It's a corporate-funded group that invites state legislators to sit with them on committees to draft model bills, which the legislators can then take back to their states. It's a very conservative group. A lot of the Stand Your Ground laws have come through there. That story, and the fact that today ALEC said it would back off of pushing the Stand Your Ground and voter suppression laws, will be some of the things we talk about.

Bloch: Does your legal background contribute to your work on the show?

Granholm: In terms of content, I'm actually the only lawyer on the staff. I always say that we should have more lawyers because when we talk about political events, there are so many legal angles. It's important to have somebody who knows how to do the research and who can interpret what a court decision might mean for broader policy. For example, right now we're talking about the Affordable Care Act. The ability to know what the Supreme Court is doing, and how to look at Paul Ryan's deficit proposal in light of obligations to fund Medicaid and Medicare, is extremely important.

Bloch: In general, what advice would you give an undergraduate student who's thinking about going into politics?

Granholm: If someone wants to run for office, prior knowledge of how a system or a nation is governed—who makes the rules and how the rules are made—is invaluable. In addition, having the knowledge and the skill to articulate and craft a persuasive argument is critical. Does that mean that law school is the only path? Of course not. But the foundation of everything in public office from knowing the difference between Medicaid, Medicare, and Social Security to how governmental immunity works all stem from a basic foundation of state and country. You have to know how to dive into those concepts.

Now, I don't want to prejudice someone to go into law believing that other disciplines are not equally valid for a career in politics. Other disciplines are truly interesting and unique, and they bring out facets and angles that are extremely valuable to public service. People often have backgrounds in medicine, math, and business. Law is a uniquely apt path to take, but it's by no means the only one.

Bloch: And do you have any more advice for a student who's thinking about law school in general?

Granholm: The nice thing about law school is that it provides a foundation for any path. It's not just a credential, it's an understanding of how the world works. That's something you might not be able to acquire anywhere else.

Interview IX
THE SPORTS AGENT

Leigh Steinberg

Leigh Steinberg is a sports agent and lawyer for some of the most successful athletes and coaches in football, basketball, baseball, hockey, boxing, golf, and more. He is a graduate of the University of California, Berkeley (1970) and UC Berkeley School of Law (1973). Steinberg has represented clients such as Steve Young, Troy Aikman, Steve Bartkowski, Warren Moon, Ben Roethlisberger, and Oscar de la Hoya, and is often credited as the real-life inspiration for Tom Cruise's character in the Academy Award-winning film, *Jerry Maguire*. He currently teaches sports law at the University of California, Irvine School of Law and runs Steinberg Sports & Entertainment.

Bloch: Can you tell me about your childhood?

Steinberg: I grew up in West Los Angeles, where my father was a high school principal. He had two core values: one was to treasure relationships, especially family, and the second was to be a force for change in the world—to help people who couldn't help themselves. Money was never a big part of that.

I went for a year to UCLA before transferring to Berkeley for my undergraduate education. I ended up student body President in 1970, right when Reagan was Governor. I started at Boalt [UC Berkeley's School of Law] in September '70.

Bloch: What sparked your interest in law?

Steinberg: When I grew up there were all sorts of lawyer shows: *The Defenders, Harry Mason, Jen for the Defense*... I always knew I wanted to be a lawyer, but my thought was to be a courtroom lawyer, a Clarence Darrow, fighting for the down-trodden. It was only when I got to law school that I realized there were all these business courses and that the courtroom stuff wasn't for me. In general, going to law school was never much of a conscious choice; it was always there. I saw it as a tool to try and make a positive difference in the world.

Bloch: Holding those values going into law school, what was your experience actually like?

Steinberg: The law school experience was a shock. In college, there's really only a few papers and a final to do for each course. If you go to most of your classes and keep up with your studies, you can pull it all together. In law school, you have to be in class every single day. I was a voracious reader, and as an undergraduate, I did the classwork and extra credit, just because I loved to read. In law school, the equivalent of that extra credit work is just keeping up with your mandatory assignments.

The way you're taught in law school is also different than the way an undergraduate education is taught. In law school, the professor, using the Socratic method, will ask you a whole series of questions. No matter how great your answer and the erudite wisdom it might hold, it is never sufficient. Also, instead of teaching the law as memorizing facts, you're using a casebook and you have to ferret out from the case what the principles of the law actually are.

They often say, "The first year they scare you, the second year they work you, and the third year they bore you." It's definitely true.

Berkeley at that time focused only on the principles of law. We had no pragmatic, practical skills. For example, we had no idea how to set up a law office or how to recruit clients. Unless you worked in a law office over the summer, you had no idea how to do much of anything. We were almost trained to be judges. Now they have all the active projects in the community, where people are actually learning real life practical experience.

Bloch: What about the courses and the grading?

Steinberg: I was completely baffled as to what all those courses were. Why were we studying civil procedure and property and the UCC [Uniform Commercial Code]? I was so naïve at one level that I really thought law school was just criminal law. I realized there was a whole business aspect to it as well.

As for grading, we had a system that's different than today. Students were still very bright and competitive, but we were judged according to a TML system. Top, middle, low. The point to it was that in a class you were very good in, you could compete for the top 15%—the equivalent of an A. If it was something you didn't enjoy as much, you would be one of the 70% in the middle. That made it a little better.

Something that's still common in law school today is that until you get back your first set of exam results, you have no idea whether or not you're actually getting the material. There's a fair amount of tension in the first semester because you're not sure if you're understanding the information in a form that can be regurgitated back on a test.

Bloch: Is that something that's starting to change?

Steinberg: I think different schools have different philosophies. I'm teaching a class on Sports and Entertainment Law at UC Irvine Law School this year. I'm not even giving them a final. It's going to be a mock negotiation instead.

Bloch: How did you transition after law school to go into the career that you have now?

Steinberg: I went through interviews and I had a series of offers in civil litigation, the DA's office, television news, and politics. I had pretty much decided that I would go work in the Alameda County DA. I wanted to get trial experience.

When I found out I passed the bar, I headed overseas for some time. When I was in Egypt traveling, I jumped into the Nile and ended up getting very sick. I spent the next six weeks at a British hospital, where I went from 170 pounds to 125 pounds. When I got back home in '74 I couldn't take any job offers because I needed to get my strength back.

In March of '75, Steve Bartkowski was the first pick in the first round of the NFL draft, and he asked me to represent him. I was brimming with legal experience, never having practiced before, and I had the very first pick in the first round of the draft in a year where the World Football League was competing against the National Football League. We got the largest rookie contract in NFL history. We eclipsed the previous standard bearers who were O.J. Simpson and Joe Namath, with a miraculous $600,000 deal for six years. That was my very first day in the job.

I remember arriving in Atlanta, and there were police lights flashing in the sky. A huge crowd is pressed against a police line, and the first thing we hear is—like for a movie premiere—"We interrupt *The Johnny Carson Show* to bring you a special news bulletin. Steve Bartkowski and Leigh Steinberg have just arrived in the Atlanta airport! Switch you live for an in-depth interview."

It was then I realized the idol worship and veneration that athletes held, and I saw the opportunity to work with athletes, who could permeate the perceptual screen that people put up against authority figures like politicians or police. Athletes could get through, so I saw my role as two-fold. My first responsibility was to stimulate the best in the young men I worked with, to teach them to nurture a sense of self-respect. The second is about being a part of a community where values withstand the test of time. If an athlete went back to the high school, collegiate, and professional communities he was a part of and retraced his roots, he could set up a role model program that would know him for the quality of his character.

Bloch: Which specific programs did you help put into motion?

Steinberg: The first program was called Kicks for Critters. Rolf Benirschke, the place kicker of the Chargers, gave money to the Fund for Endangered Species at the San Diego Zoo for every field goal he kicked. There were posters and pledge cards all around the city. We could raise consciousness for endangered species, and lots of money. That was the first program that tied a player's performance on the field with charitable giving off the field. Now you see those programs everywhere.

Over the years, about 120 scholarship funds at a collegiate level have been set up as well. Troy Aikman and Eric Karros repaid their scholarships to UCLA, Steve Young to BYU, and more. I did a series of those. At a pro level I challenged each athlete to find something in their own lives they would like to tackle so that they could leave a legacy. We started foundations with leading clinical figures, business pioneers, and community leaders.

Bloch: And what was it like to be an agent with a law degree?

Steinberg: There wasn't much sports law back then. There was no guaranteed right of representation either. A general manager could say, "We don't deal with agents."

I saw the whole concept of agency in a very different way. The real battle was not labor versus management. The battle the NFL had was with baseball, basketball, home box office, Walt Disney World, and every other form of discretionary entertainment spending. If that was true, then my job was to not engage in acrimonious personal negotiations because bad discussions or collective bargaining agreements alienate the fans. I tried to take the fans into account.

Bloch: How do you think that your law school experiences helped you leave this huge legacy on the sports world?

Steinberg: Law school did teach a certain way of thinking, although the skills I really needed in those first negotiations were political and psychological skills. The ability to get into the heart and mind of another person and understand what their greatest dreams and aspirations, hopes, and fears are is invaluable.

As for class in particular, there was nothing that transformational, because in reality, if you were going to do contracts, you had to go back and relearn how to do contracts anyway. I did have terrific professors, and certain classes like tax law were helpful. The business law classes I took were probably the most useful.

Bloch: Looking back, do you feel as though you made the right decision going to law school?

Steinberg: It is not totally necessary in the field of sports representation. Agents can come from all sorts of backgrounds, but I didn't know that back then.

Bloch: What type of advice would you give to an undergraduate student who's thinking about going into the sports world?

Steinberg: Go to business school, or maybe law school. Both disciplines can be helpful. At the end of the day, athletes are looking for someone with a specific skill set that can add something to their lives. It's not important to know the stats from the 1902 World Series. Have something—branding, endorsements, contract negotiation, incorporation—that is a really practical, tangible asset. I think the best degree to do might be a joint JD/MBA.

Here's the point: remember in *The Wizard of Oz* when the scarecrow feels dumb the entire movie, and at the end he gets a diploma and starts to elucidate all the world's great thoughts? Well, the essence of sports representation is that it's hypercompetitive. For every one who succeeds there are thousands and thousands of people who tried to do it. So I think it's wise to have a point of personal branding that delineates a specific skill set. It may be of comfort to potential clients and their parents if you have a law degree.

My own view is that the more exposure you can get to different issues that may come up, like business or marketing, the better. Remember that sports, even for an attorney, is much bigger than representation. It's sports television, sports marketing, it's working for teams and leagues and universities. Sports television alone is a massive field. For example, my former assistant Robert Hacker later became Vice President of Legal Affairs for Fox Sports Television. The point is that there are careers to be found in all those things. There are new technologies on the Internet and new apps that have to do with health and fitness. We do sports-related content, motion pictures, television, video games, mobile apps, and Internet apps.

I think the key is to have a dream, a passion, a vision for how this can be a better place, and there must be the belief that one's work is having a positive impact on clients and the world.

Interview X
THE REAR ADMIRAL

James E. McPherson

Two-star Rear Admiral James McPherson was the 39th Judge Advocate General of the United States Navy from 2004-2006 in the Judge Advocate General's Corps (JAG Corps). He is a graduate of San Diego State University (1977), received his Juris Doctor degree from the University of San Diego School of Law (1981), and was awarded a Master of Laws degree in Military Law from The Judge Advocate General's School (1991). During his military career, he was awarded the Distinguished Service Medal, the Legion of Merit, and the Meritorious Service Medal. He currently serves as the Executive Director of the National Association of Attorneys General.

Bloch: Take me back to how you grew up.

McPherson: I'm from Escondido, California. I grew up there, and went on to San Diego State University for undergrad, and then to San Diego School of Law.

Bloch: What did you study at San Diego State?

McPherson: Public administration, so how to be a bureaucrat. It turned out well for me. I didn't have law school in mind. I actually went to work for the Navy as a civil servant for a year before I applied to law school.

Bloch: When did you first get interested in law?

McPherson: As a kid I was interested in law enforcement more than anything else. I actually applied to the Los Angeles Police Department when I was 20-years-old. I took the tests and everything, but I ended up going to San Diego State instead, and I'm glad I did. It was there that my interest in law enforcement changed into an interest in the law. When I went to work for the Navy, before law school, I worked for a great guy who had been a civil servant for about 40 years. However, watching him convinced me that I didn't want to be a civil servant for the rest of my life, so I took the LSAT and applied to law school.

Bloch: How would you describe your law school experience?

McPherson: It was an excellent experience. Although academically San Diego isn't in the top 20, it's probably number one in self-discipline. The choice is go to class and study in the afternoon, or walk two blocks down to Mission Bay [a popular San Diego beach]. With that temptation you had to discipline yourself to go to class and study. It was also challenging, but law school was a good experience. I enjoyed it.

Bloch: What was the toughest part of your law school experience?

McPherson: The first year. Everyone will say that. That's when you learn the tricks of the trade. In the first year the faculty tend to give you more homework than you can possibly do. The reasoning behind that is to teach you how to do triage. How to make decisions about what's important to read word for word and what you can skim over. In the first year the reading assignments are crushing. The second year was comparable to the first or second year of undergrad, and the third year you can almost sleep through.

Bloch: Is the biggest value of going to law school learning that self-discipline and how to figure out what's important in the material?

McPherson: Yes, but law schools today are having some real challenges. They are becoming more like trade schools. They're trying to teach people how to be attorneys, and that's not what law school did when I went through it. Law schools then really taught how to think and analyze and look at factual situations and find the important issues. I think today the market demands more from law schools in respect to coming out of it and being able to practice the law immediately. Back when I went through law school, you graduated and then became an associate at a firm or wherever you were working. There was a long mentoring process and apprenticeship that went on. Today, law firms—and the government too in fact—can't afford to do that any longer. You have to be able to practice law from the day you step out of your law school.

Bloch: Is that a good thing in your opinion?

McPherson: It remains to be seen what the market has done to law school. There are people on both sides of that equation and good arguments to be made for both sides. I enjoyed the intellectual challenge of law school more than I would have enjoyed the trade school aspect of how to draft a will or how to do a deposition. Typically you learn those in practice from more senior attorneys in the firm, but today, that's changing radically.

Bloch: What was your career path after law school?

McPherson: I joined the Navy during my first year of law school. That was prompted by the economics of the situation at the time. In the late 70's the economy was worse than it is now. I had friends—third year students who were graduating—who didn't have jobs. They were going to work bussing tables. I decided I needed to find a job while I was still in law school. So I thought about the services, and I went to every one of the four main branches. At the time, the Navy was the only one that offered a student program. That is, you could apply and become a member of the Navy JAG Corps, in the reserves, while still in law school.

The other three services, at the time, required you to have passed the bar. The Navy was the only one that offered you the prospect of having a guaranteed job upon graduation, and that's the reason I went with them. My initial experience in the Navy was litigation, which, for the first three or four years is very typical. Specifically, criminal law practice.

My next assignment was as a legal advisor to Navy commanders. I was assigned to a Naval Air Station in the Philippines for three years. Then I went on board a ship, the USS Theodore Roosevelt, for two years. I enjoyed that a whole lot. I didn't make it a career decision until I had been in for about ten years. I just woke up one morning and discovered I'd been in the Navy for that long, and I thought, "Gee, this is a career now!" So I guess you could say I kind of backed into it.

After the carrier I went on to get my master's degree in law from The Judge Advocate General's School in Charlottesville, Virginia and then went back into the courtroom, which is unusual. Then, I was stationed at the Pentagon for over ten years as legal advisor to various Navy commanders.

Bloch: What was it like being the head of the entire JAG Corps?

McPherson: It was interesting. I didn't get a chance to practice law anymore. Even senior attorneys at a large law firm still practice law, but when you're in the government and move up in rank, whether it be in the military or civil service, you tend to leave behind the practice of law and you manage and lead law efforts instead.

For me that's what I did when I got into the senior ranks in the Navy. The most important decisions I made were personnel decisions. I was deciding what the future of the Navy JAG Corps would look like. The people we were sending to career enhancing positions or the ones we were promoting, things like that. I was there when we started sending people to Iraq. At its height, I had probably 60 or 70 attorneys in Iraq, and maybe half that number of paralegal support. The big responsibility for me was deciding who I was sending over there. Quite frankly, not to sound melodramatic, but what worried me was getting that phone call in the middle of the night that one of my people had been wounded or killed. While I was in there I had two people who were wounded in action. They came back to Bethesda and I'd get to see them there and tell them how much we appreciate what they did, and how thankful we were that they didn't get killed.

It's very sobering. What I didn't want to have to do was get on the phone and have to visit a mom or dad or spouse and tell them that I was the guy that decided to send their son or daughter, husband or wife, mother or father, off to Iraq, and they weren't coming home.

Bloch: Given that you weren't actually practicing law at the upper levels, what part of law school helped you deal with that type of job?

McPherson: One of the things that I discovered when I first reported to the Pentagon to work for senior officers as a legal advisor was developing the skill of taking an investigative report—or any sort of report—that was several pages or volumes long, and distilling it down to a single page.

The ability to read through a 20-page investigation, or 200-page investigation, and distill it down to one page using the facts, the law, and then my recommendations was a skill that I learned in my first year of law school. The analysis of factual situations, the ability to pick up important issues, and then the expression of those issues in a way that's clear and not full of jargon is critical. The audience I was writing to were senior naval officers who weren't attorneys. I would say the experience of analyzing and being able to come up with succinct arguments was a skill that I learned in law school that I didn't apply until later on.

Bloch: What piece of advice would you give to an undergraduate in college who's thinking about becoming an attorney in the JAG Corps?

McPherson: A couple things. None of the JAG Corps are alike in how they recruit or what they require. There are five branches of services, two of which are unique, the Marines and the Coast Guard, in that their JAG are line officers. They will have assignments that are not legal in nature. They will be at a safety office or headquarters for usually every third assignment. They'll go off into what they call a dissociative tour, which is when they do something that has no relevance to law whatsoever. They're all typical Coast Guard officers at that time.

I worked with a Coast Guard JAG one time who came to work for me when I was in Norfolk. His previous assignment was as a commanding officer of a cutter. The guy out there on the coast doing anti-drug operations with his ship and a crew of some 40 people was an attorney, a judge advocate. The same thing is true of the Marine Corps, they are line officers who specialize in law. Two out of every three assignments will be legal-related, and then the third assignment in a nine- or ten-year span will not be law-related. They may be a supply officer or they may command a company. Those two are outliers.

The other three, the main ones—Army, Navy, and Air Force—you're a staff officer and that's all you'll do. You'll do legal duties your entire tour. Now it can vary doing court martial work, and usually, initial assignment for all three is doing court martials, and then they go off and specialize in something else in a legal advisor capacity.

There are a couple things to keep in mind. Usually for the first two, three, or four years, pay in the military will be competitive with pay in the civilian community. But at the four- or five-year point your classmates in law school who went to private firms, or even those who are working for the federal government, will get past you and you'll never see them again. It's just the way it is with pay scales. They recruit differently.

Bloch: How does recruitment differ across branches?

McPherson: The Big 3 will fill their yearly quotas with first year students. Most of them are what are called "unfunded," but you're in the reserves. That's how they'll fill up. If you're a second or third year student, if you go to any of those three seeking to get into their JAG Corps, they're probably full already. They'll already have filled their quota with first year law students, so you have to make that decision early on.

All the services now visit campuses. At some time during your first year, there will be a visit from the Army, Navy, or Air Force Corps; we send JAG officers to career days. Talk to them, and get their literature. It's very competitive. The market now is such that all three services can usually pick one out of every six to ten applicants.

Selection is largely based upon your LSAT score, the law school you attend, your undergraduate GPA, and any other extracurricular activities you can bring in. Oftentimes now the services are selecting people who have had some job experience too. That's not to say that someone who went straight to law school is handicapped, but it's something they now often consider because the competition is so keen.

Bloch: Let's say someone is finishing high school or starting their undergraduate studies and they already know they want to go to the JAG Corps. What are some things you would recommend for them to do when getting to college?

McPherson: If you're not an English major, take a lot of English classes. It sounds sort of counterintuitive. You may think that my recommendation would be a Political Science major or something like that, and yes, you can do that, but the key is to be well-rounded and well-read. In order to be successful in the JAG Corps you need to be able to read, analyze, and think critically. One of the ways you do that is by getting into literature. I'd recommend to take a lot of English and writing courses.

Also, be heavily involved in extracurricular activities. A selection board will want to see that you're a well-rounded undergraduate, whether it be athletics, community service, or something else. Get involved with clubs. If you have the opportunity to go overseas for a semester to study, do it. Get that breadth and experience. The applicants that bring the greatest experience to bear, as well as a good GPA, are more likely than others to be selected.

Bloch: If you could go back, would you take the same route or do anything differently?

McPherson: I'd take the route I did. Oftentimes a lot of it was luck, quite frankly. What I found attractive was that with military experience, you're doing something different all the time. Even though I was in the same job for two or three years, I knew that I'd soon be moving on. I found that very attractive, but not all people find it that way. Some people are more comfortable being in the same office, the same job for their entire careers. That wasn't me. I wanted to go out and see things and do things. If someone has that interest in working and traveling overseas, the military is a great opportunity. That's what you'll do. You'll wake up in the morning and find yourself in the Philippines or in Italy or in Baghdad. There's a lot of adventure to it.

Interview XI
THE ENTREPRENEUR

Todd R. Wagner

Todd Wagner is the co-founder of Broadcast.com, which he sold with partner Mark Cuban to Yahoo! for $5.7 billion in 1999. He graduated from Indiana University (1983) and received his Juris Doctor degree from the University of Virginia School of Law (1986). Wagner manages his own charitable foundation, The Todd Wagner Foundation, which is dedicated to improving the lives of at-risk children and inner-city communities by increasing access to technology, education, and capital. In addition to his philanthropic work, Wagner has built the Wagner/Cuban business portfolio, which includes 2929 Entertainment, HDNet Films, Magnolia Pictures, Landmark Theatres, and ownership stakes in the Dallas Mavericks, The Weinstein Company, and Lions Gate Entertainment.

Bloch: Can you take me back to how you grew up?

Wagner: I grew up in the Midwest in a steel mill town called Gary, Indiana. It's probably best known because Michael Jackson was born there. My mom was a homemaker, and my father was a dentist who put himself through school on the GI Bill after having served in World War II. I lived in Gary until I went to college at Indiana University, where I studied accounting.

Bloch: Why did you decide to study accounting?

Wagner: I didn't really know what else to study. I thought business sounded the most interesting. There were three majors within the business field: marketing, finance, and accounting. I was told accounting was the most difficult and the one that would most likely land me a job, so I chose to study that.

Bloch: Where did your interest in law first come from?

Wagner: I passed through business school and took the CPA exam. I knew that accounting wasn't something I wanted to pursue as a career, but I had an internship with KPMG in Chicago and it was nice, even though it wasn't for me.

My parents told me to go and get an advanced degree. The only thing I'd ever heard about an advanced degree in those days was studying to become a doctor, dentist, or lawyer. I wasn't very interested in the sciences, so that ruled out being a dentist or a doctor. That just left law school.

It wasn't that I had any desire to be a lawyer—I didn't think it was going to be my life's work. It was more like, "This is just another hurdle to get over, another degree that will hopefully be helpful in my life's journey. I'll try and get into the best law school I can and kind of take it from there."

Bloch: Heading to law school with that mindset, what was your experience like?

Wagner: I was a Midwestern kid. I'd gone to public schools my entire life. I hadn't really had a lot of the advantages that some of the kids I went to law school with had. I went to law school at the University of Virginia. Most of my classmates had either gone there for undergrad or they'd gone to an Ivy League school. It was a whole new level of people. It's kind of like sports—at each level the players get better. If you're good in high school, then you play in college. If you're good in college, then you might be able to play with the pros, but at each level the competition gets more intense. That's what I experienced.

UVA was a top 10 law school. These were kids who had a lot of private school education. It's like they were prepped their entire lives to be lawyers. They had a lot of good study habits that I didn't have. I went to school with Chief Justice Rehnquist's daughter, I went to school with one of the Kennedy's—it was this whole new world I'd never seen before.

Having said that, Charlottesville is a great place to go to school, and I still keep in touch with a lot of my classmates. But I knew even then that being a lawyer would not be what I was going to do for the rest of my life. But I'm not a quitter and I don't stop, so I kept going, got through law school, and passed the bar exam.

Bloch: What was the biggest value of getting a law degree?

Wagner: I practiced law for eight years before I quit and became an entrepreneur. Those years of law school and being a lawyer turned out to be magnificent for what eventually became my real aptitude and my real career. So I kind of stumbled into all of it, but my business undergraduate degree and my law degree turned out to be fabulous.

But it's not for everybody. As you well know, there are some entrepreneurs who know at the age of 18 or 19 that traditional routes aren't for them. For your generation, it's Mark Zuckerberg. For mine, it's Steve Jobs and Bill Gates. The guys who went to college for a year or two, and then dropped out to start a business.

I think most people want something to fall back on, and so for me, I wasn't ready at the age of 20 to say, "I know exactly what I want to do, how to start a business, and what that business ought to look like." For me, I felt I needed the additional education, training, and my own personal experience. By the time I got to be 33, I was more than ready. I felt like I knew what I wanted to do and I just needed an opportunity to go do it.

Bloch: What motivated you to join Mark Cuban and launch Audionet?

Wagner: Mark and I were college friends and knew each other pretty well. He was one of the only entrepreneurs I knew because most folks would become either a lawyer, doctor, banker, or something else. Back in those days people didn't really gravitate toward technology—there was no real technology industry. It was inhabited by the "supergeeks" who put Local Area Networks together. There wasn't a lot of entrepreneurial zest out there.

But Mark was one of those guys. He had started a business out of college, sold it, and successfully been an entrepreneur. That was a path that I thought I wanted to get on. Mark and I sat down and we talked about some different things and he said, "You know, if you come up with a cool idea, I'd do it with you." So that was the genesis of Audionet, which became Broadcast.com.

Bloch: You worked at Broadcast.com for five years. Can you take me through the process of what happened with the company?

Wagner: I was the CEO of the company so it was an unbelievable experience. I got to put into practice everything I dreamed of, which was to start a business, hire employees, build a sales staff, build a marketing team, and understand the technology aspects. Starting something from the ground up from no employees to 500, it was an experience of a lifetime and it was a job that Mark and I always tease about. No one would have hired us to do what we did. They would have hired someone else, but as it turns out, we think it was a really good decision it was us!

The way the business and startup community works is that the starters of the company don't usually last long. They're not the right guys to take it to the next level or investors don't feel that they have the skill set to do it. I believe that because Mark and I had really complementary skill sets—plus we were a little older—we brought a whole lot more experience to the table. Mark had already built a business and I'd been a CPA and lawyer for eight years, so we had some real background in businesses and what made them hum. I think that was a part of what allowed us to be successful and to frankly, keep our jobs, if you will.

Bloch: Do you think your experience in law school helped?

Wagner: I think both law school and business school helped. No question having a business degree was useful because I had taken so many finance and accounting courses. However, I think law school was also quite beneficial. What law school teaches you is the ability to argue both sides of an issue and understand things in more of an abstract way. If you allow it to, it gives you more creative thinking. Creativity doesn't necessarily mean being an artist. There's also business creativity. I think law school taught me some of those things and helped me to apply them.

All these years later, since Broadcast.com, I've had yet another career and another decade of being in the media, movie, and startup industries. All the lessons I've learned were very valuable. But there's no lesson better than the one of actually doing it yourself—of actually sitting at the wheel of a startup and having to drive it. That's a lesson that can't be taught at any school or in any classroom.

Bloch: Given your wild success, how did the move to The Todd Wagner Foundation occur?

Wagner: When we sold our business, I was 38-years-old. It's a blessing and a curse having the amount of wealth that Mark and I had. You don't want to retire and play golf everyday. I looked for things that would still be interesting for me, knowing that I really didn't need to work any longer for just the money, I needed to work for other reasons.

First thing for me was to start my foundation. I wanted to give back because I felt so incredibly lucky. It just doesn't happen—to take a business from zero to $5.7 billion in four and a half years. I felt a real sense of duty and obligation to try and give back to people who didn't have the same opportunities that I did. We had worked hard; I put in a lot of effort, a lot of 100-hour weeks. I put all my savings into the business. I put in everything I had. Having said that, I had the opportunity to do that because I had a good education. I had a good set of parents who cared about me, and it gave me the chance to potentially succeed. I wanted to try and help others who didn't have those opportunities. And frankly, I spent the first year or two after we sold the business focused almost exclusively on the foundation. Once that got off the ground I kind of started looking around for what was next, and for me, that was the media industry. We had already touched it tangentially with Broadcast.com. I was fascinated by the movie industry. Three to four years after that, Mark and I were back in partnership again. We owned Landmark Theatres [a national theater chain], we started a distribution company, a production company, and a television network. We were back at it, both a little older and a little wiser.

Bloch: Actually, to prep for this interview, I rewatched Akeelah and the Bee and I must say I really enjoyed the movie! It's very inspiring.

Wagner: Well thank you very much. If you look close I'm actually in it. I'm the regional spelling bee judge about halfway through the movie! But anyway, it's a great movie—one that I'm really proud of. And partly why I backed it is that it's kind of the movie version of what I think we are trying to accomplish with my foundation.

Bloch: What do you hope to do in the future?

Wagner: I'm always looking for the next thing. The things that get me the most excited now are startups. I'm obviously not going to be the CEO. I don't have the time or the energy to do it, but I try to find ones that I can either advise, be an investor, or if I like it a lot, be a chairman or vice-chairman on the board. There are about three or four of those now that I'm looking at, and one or two of those I'll pick to get more deeply involved in. That's my way to stay involved with what's going on now in the Internet and technology.

Our media businesses are all profitable. We've been very creative about how we distribute movies—we've learned how to use technology to our advantage, which are all lessons we learned from Broadcast.com. I love what we're doing in that space. I sit on the Board of the American Film Institute and the Tribeca Film Festival, so those are all very fun and interesting things to me as well.

Bloch: What's one piece of advice you would give to someone my age, who's thinking about going into entrepreneurship?

Wagner: I'm going to give you a little bit of a contrarian view than what you've been told by everyone. If someone told me they were a liberal arts major and studying English or history, and they wanted to go into the business world and get an MBA, I'd say that's a great idea. But if you're already studying business and want to go on and get an MBA, it's relatively duplicative. What you'll learn in MBA school is not going to surpass what you've already learned in a quality business school. Obviously I'm biased and I never went back to get my MBA, but I did think about it.

I remember one conversation when I spoke to Mark about what I was going to do because I knew I didn't want to be a lawyer and I'd resigned from the law firm. I told him I was thinking about going back to get an MBA at Harvard because, "Gee Mark, that will open more doors." And I still remember him saying to me, "That's great, Todd. I hire MBAs."

The point of Mark's story was if you're an entrepreneur, then you're an entrepreneur. You don't need advanced degrees in order to do it. You either got it or you don't. And his point was that I already had a business undergrad degree. I already had a law degree. How many more degrees did I need?

So to be a bit of a contrarian, you may say, "Being a lawyer doesn't sound like it's for me," to which I might say to you, consider it.

Consider doing it for what you'll take and learn. There are lots of folks who went to law school and never practiced law. They used it as a springboard for other things. In the business world, whether you want to be a venture capitalist, an entrepreneur, or whatever role you think you may want to do, the ability to understand and read documents, understand legal concepts, and understand how things get drafted and what they mean is of prime importance. You could just hire a lawyer, but you better know what you're signing and you better understand what's in there, especially in the early stages of a startup.

Once you're a certain size of course you'll have a General Counsel and people to tell you what you're signing, but as someone who was in a startup, my legal background was immensely important to Mark and I during that first year or two. My ability to draft things and send it to clients made a big impact. I didn't have to wait for a lawyer to review it, sign off on it, and send it back. Not to mention the fees we saved.

Bloch: How does someone know if entrepreneurship is right for them?

Wagner: As a guy who's worn a lot of hats over the years, this is the situation you should think about: If you're the type of person who likes to drive the car, then you need to be an entrepreneur. If you're the type of person who likes to advise the one driving the car, then you want to be a consultant or venture capitalist or investment banker. You've got to understand your personality. I'm the type of guy who wants the wheel; I want to drive. Therefore, as a lawyer or any other capacity, all I was doing was advising entrepreneurs. I remember thinking, "I can do that, and I can do it better."

You've got to know yourself. Some people don't want to take the risk. They know that if they have a great undergrad degree, or they get an MBA from Harvard or Stanford, all the doors are open, and they'll make a tremendous living. I didn't have that option. I didn't have as many doors open to me. It obviously turned out OK for me, but the reality is that you have to know who you are and what you want.

I remember getting into an argument once with a VC who said, "Oh, I've got all these great companies I own, and I run this and we're doing that." And I said, "Do you *run* it?" And he said, "Well, no." So I responded, "You don't run it. You're advising him [the CEO], but he's running it. You can act all day long like they're your companies, but you're not running them." It's the difference between being a coach and a player. You can be a really hands-on coach, but you're still not on the court.

I'm obviously biased because I've been an entrepreneur, and that for me is what gets me jazzed, but for other people, that's not how they work. They want someone else to be sitting in the first chair. That just wouldn't work for me. My aptitude, my strength, my gift was being behind the wheel.

Bloch: When would someone know if they're ready to do that?

Wagner: The hard decision for anyone is to know when they're ready. As I said, not many are ready very young. I'll tell you, be young when you want to do it, but don't be so young that you're not taken seriously. There are exceptions, but those are enormous exceptions. The more likely path to success is to continue with your education, get your degree, and then if you want to be an entrepreneur, go for it.

If you're not married, all the kinds of things that allow you the freedom to work long hours—to not need very much money, to not care if you're living off pizza and beer—all those things are important.

I always ask two questions to any entrepreneur, and they always tell me exactly what I need to know. The first question: Are you willing to put in your own money? And the second question: Are you willing to quit your day job? If the answer isn't yes to both of them, they're not entrepreneurs. And that's how I always evaluate people because the ones who say, "Well, I don't want to quit my job because if it doesn't work..." That's the wrong answer. If you don't let go of the side of the pool, you're never going to swim. You have to have fear of failure. You have to have fear that you'll drown and go under, or you will not make it.

The other thing that I look for is a willingness to put your own money in. Because if the guy says, "No, I just want to raise money from angels and venture capitalists," then if the thing fails, you won't be in a lot of pain. The only way you're truly invested is if you have a big piece of your net worth in it. I'm not saying it has to be a million dollars—it might be ten thousand dollars—but I want to know that if this thing doesn't work, it's going to hurt you. That's what I look for.

Bloch: Any final advice?

Wagner: You know, it's funny. I get hundreds of emails a day from people and normally I don't respond the way I did to yours, but it caught my eye. One thing I've wished I had when I was your age was people giving me their two cents about the path.

Obviously you can ignore everything I say and disagree with it, and that's your prerogative, but I didn't have anybody to talk to for advice. I just kind of had to stumble and bumble through, and as I said, yes, it turned out OK for me, but there might have been a more direct path that would've been a little easier if I had someone to talk to. And that's why I applaud you. I think there will be folks your age who at least want to discuss: Should I be a lawyer? Should I get an MBA? What are the pros and cons? What should I think about?

I had a rare experience because I've led a business with one employee and I've led as many as 5,000 employees too. I've seen no revenues. I've seen a billion dollars per year. I've experienced so much and I've seen all ends of the spectrum. I feel like I have a really unique perspective, especially because I was a lawyer and a business major, and so I have a lot of input to provide. Finding people who can give you advice is one of the smartest things you can do.

Epilogue

First, thank you for reading *Learning From Precedent.* I hope you enjoyed the book and that at least one (and hopefully more) of the interviews spoke to you profoundly, as they did for me. I hope this book has helped you decide whether you too should go to law school.

Personally, I took away a great deal from each one of these incredible individuals. Chairman Ruder's path to the SEC taught me to capitalize on every opportunity available. Take the opportunities that will allow your wildest dreams to come true. Governor Granholm's anecdote on protesting Apartheid made me realize that the freethinking attitude so common in college students across the United States can persist throughout a lifetime. A desire to change the world for better need never end. Judge Fogel reminded me that no matter how heated a legal matter may get, and how different two sides may seem, never forget that the person opposite from you is still a person. Respect his/her approach and understand that consensus is created through communication. From Mr. Layne I learned to branch out from my immediate interests. The law touches every field, and the more knowledge you have, the more value you can offer to your firm and to your clients. Ms. Herman showed us that everyone deserves a chance. Sometimes, protecting the greater good is more important than our personal thoughts or feelings on a matter. Mr. Steinberg attested to the importance of mentorship. No matter your age or profession, everyone should aspire to give back to the communities of which they are a part.

Each interviewee showed me that success comes in following a passion and truly believing that daily actions make a difference. No matter what each interviewee chose to pursue, each one expressed two things: knowing what they wanted and why they wanted it.

One of the most impactful discussions I had was with Mr. Wagner. During my time speaking with him, I was able to share sentiments about where my life is headed and what I hope to accomplish. Speaking with him, and empowered with knowledge from other interviewees, has led me to the goal of pursuing a joint JD/MBA in the future.

I hope that you take the next step to create your own "book" of this sort. Be proactive and create your own list of interviewees who will level with you. Talk to them. Listen to them. Learn from them. It's not simply about interviewing—it's about engaging. And, if you have focus and fire, you can reach the vision you've set for yourself.

Resources

If you're looking for more resources regarding law school, you have come to the right section of *Learning From Precedent*. Of course, online resources about law school abound. My favorite destination is Top-Law-Schools.com; it is one of the best places for comprehensive law school information, and they have almost everything you'll ever need to know about applying to law schools, how to do well once you're there, and more.

For current law school rankings, I recommend:
http://grad-schools.usnews.rankingsandreviews.com/best-graduate-schools/top-law-schools

For more information about the current Law School Admissions Test (LSAT), I recommend:
http://www.lsac.org/JD/LSAT/about-the-LSAT.asp - This is the online home of the Law School Admission Council.

For more information about Law School Admissions Test (LSAT) preparation, I recommend:
http://lsatblog.blogspot.com/ - This is a go-to website managed by an LSAT tutor who gives out comprehensive advice.
http://www.princetonreview.com/law-school.aspx
http://www.testmasters.com/lsat.html
http://www.kaptest.com/LSAT/Home/index.html

That said, to me, the most valuable information about law school has come from personal interactions with faculty and fellow students. Consider joining a pre-law organization or group on your college campus. Check out your college career center as they can provide much guidance. Finally, the Legal Studies, Political Science, English, and other humanities or social sciences majors often have abundant resources about law school too.

The website for the book, www.LearningFromPrecedent.com, includes more information and links that you may find helpful as well.

Acknowledgements

Thank you so much to each person who helped in the creation of *Learning from Precedent*. First, I'd like to thank everyone I had a chance to interview: Jennifer Granholm, Kenneth Dam, David Ruder, Leigh Steinberg, Roger Wolfson, Jonathan Layne, Sean Dean, Jeremy Fogel, James McPherson, Susan Herman, and Todd Wagner. I learned so much from each of your personal stories and anecdotes, and your advice has provided me with a clearer vision of what I hope to accomplish in my future. Your willingness to provide insight and wisdom into your respective professions has contributed to an invaluable guide for countless others who hope to achieve similar positions of success and influence.

Next, my family. Doreen—this book was written because of you. Your own book served as inspiration for the creation of this one, and thank you for the help you gave me on every facet of it. You are the greatest big sister that a little brother could ask for. My mother, Sophia—thank you for being an integral part of the editing process and demanding that I always do my best. To my little sister Adele, now that both me and Doreen have written books, I expect to be helping you on yours soon! My dad, Simon. I appreciate greatly the advice you gave me on the business sections of *Learning from Precedent*.

To all the brothers at my fraternity, Sigma Nu, I owe you for keeping the house (relatively) quiet during my interviews. Thank you to Cody DeCamp, Nathan Miller, Russell Miller, Andrew Ayala, Jecht Tsang, and my three littles, Ryan Coleman, Stuart Wilson, and Ben Greenberg.

A special thanks to brothers of Sigma Nu who are also in Phi Alpha Delta, the pre-law fraternity: Hayden McFarlane, Kevin Gibson, Ashwin Aravind, and Brian Weissenberg. I appreciate your support and unique perspectives on this project.

Erin Delaney and Emrin Dhatt: Thank you for being the greatest best friends a guy could have. Since the very beginning of our Phi Alpha Delta LIT semester you two have always been there for me—from 2 a.m. Pancho's dinner runs to weekend excursions to Lodi.

To my friends in Phi Alpha Delta and the Tau class, thank you for launching my interest in law. Special thanks here to Ryan Kwock, Rachel Chenoweth, and my LIT parents, Krystie Mak, Jordan Giannoni, and Annie Zanobini.

Thank you to Jessica Maley for the awesome cover design. I appreciate all the long hours you spent working on it, and it certainly turned out great.

Thank you to every other person who contributed to this project, especially to Sarah Zearfoss for her remarkable Foreword essay that so perfectly captured the era and the essence of this project. Thank you also to Helene Kim, Jamie Brown, Andrew Marston, Shelby Layne, and Megan Wilcox-Fogel; each of you helped me with a key piece of this work. I couldn't have done it without you.

About Michael Bloch

Michael Bloch is an undergraduate at the University of California, Berkeley, Class of 2013. He studies Business Administration at the Walter A. Haas School of Business and Political Science. Bloch serves as President of the Beta Psi chapter of Sigma Nu fraternity and is a member of the Phi Alpha Delta chapter at Cal.

Made in the USA
Monee, IL
04 November 2026

67378033R00059